THE HANDBOOK
for
Pastors' and Ministers' Wives

A. P. Wyfe

First in the Pastor's Wife series of Books

THE HANDBOOK *for Pastors' and Ministers' Wives*

A. P. Wyfe

First in the Pastor's Wife series of Books

Published by:The KR Company, publishers of Christian Books
110 West 9th Street Box 321
Wilmington, DE 19801

Printed in the USA by: Morris Publishing
3212 E. Highway 30
Kearney, NE 68847   1-800-650-7888

ISBN 0-9712943-0-5

Table of Contents

Author's Note

I have endeavored to write a book that will not only be a working tool for pastors' and ministers' wives, but will also encourage you to examine yourselves as Christian human beings, and as people whose actions have a definite effect on the lives of others.

Nowhere in this book will you find the words "are you like this woman?" However, with every godly and ungodly example presented on these pages, you should be asking this question of yourself.

I have not limited the Scriptures in this book to Scriptures that simply use the word "wife," but have chosen to include those Scriptures that pertain to women, mothers, types of women, and types of people.

The type of woman that you are determines the type of wife and mother that you are as well. The type of person you are says much about the type of Christian you are.

I would like to make it perfectly clear that I believe the Bible to be the Word of God, and as it is written in 2 Timothy 3:16, I believe that "all scripture is given by inspiration of God, and is profitable for doctrine, for reproof, for correction, for instruction in righteousness:"

A. P. Wyfe
1999

Who can find a virtuous woman? For her price is far above rubies.

The heart of her husband doth safely trust in her, so that he shall have no need of spoil.

She will do him good and not evil all the days of her life.

She seeketh wool, and flax, and worketh willingly with her hands.

She is like the merchant's ships; she bringeth her food from afar.

She riseth also while it is yet night, and giveth meat to her household, and a portion to her maidens.

She considereth a field, and buyeth it: with the fruit of her hands she planteth a vineyard.

She girdeth her loins with strength, and strengtheneth her arms.

She perceiveth that her merchandise is good: her candle goeth not out by night.

She layeth her hands to the spindle, and her hands hold the distaff.

She streatcheth out her hand to the poor; yea, she reacheth forth
her hands to the needy.

She is not afraid of the snow for her household: for all her household are clothed with scarlet.

She maketh herself coverings of tapestry; her clothing is silk and purple.

Her husband is known in the gates, when he sitteth among the elders of the land.

She maketh fine linen, and selleth it; and delivereth girdles unto the merchant.

Strength and honor are her clothing; and she shall rejoice in time to come.

She openeth her mouth with wisdom; and in her tongue is the law of kindness.

She looketh well to the ways of her household, and eateth not the bread of idleness.

Her children arise up and call her blessed; her husband also, and he praiseth her.

Many daughters have done virtuously, but thou excellest them all.

Favour is deceitful, and beauty is vain: but a woman that feareth the Lord, she shall be praised.

Give her of the fruit of her hands; and let her own works praise her in the gate.

Proverbs 31:10-31

Dedication

This Book is dedicated to God, for allowing me the privilege of being called into His ministry.

This book is further dedicated to the memory of Mother Laura Steward, the quintessential missionary.

Mother Steward died at the age of 105 years old. She was saved at the age of sixteen, and never faltered from the course that God set before her. She forsook all others to follow Jesus. There were times when she was chastised by her acquaintances, and talked about by her church family because she put God ahead of all others. She gave of herself in all that she did; she possessed the gift of faith that allowed her to believe that no task was too great for God to accomplish.

At the age of eighty-seven, she traveled to Haiti to establish a mission, and by the time she had reached her nineties, she had also established a school and a church. She continued to travel to Haiti until her death.

Her funeral was a celebration of a life lived in Christ.

"I have fought a good fight, I have finished my course, I have kept the faith:

Henceforth there is laid up for me a crown of righteousness, which the Lord, the righteous judge, shall give me at that day: and not to me only, but unto all them also that love His appearing."   2 Tim. 4:7-8

I hope that at the appointed time, the same can be said about me.

I am grateful for having known her, and I am grateful that God placed her in the path of two baby Christians to teach and to strengthen us.

As always, love to my family and friends for their support and encouragement.

Foreword

I wrote this book in the name of A. P. Wyfe, because I could be *any* pastor's wife, in *any* Christian denomination, in *any* church, in *any* town, *any*where in the world.

I hope this book will encourage EVERY pastor and minister's wife to rise to the calling of the ministry of help mate with renewed strength and vigor.

Some of us feel unworthy, and some of us feel overwhelmed. Many of us feel like the proverbial fish out of water. All of us feel at some time or another, that our jobs are thankless. I say to you be encouraged, for God has chosen you especially, to do a job that only you can do.

A. P. Wyfe

Acknowledgments

I would like to acknowledge all of the pastor's wives, evangelists, and godly women who have loved me, shared with me, befriended me, and taught me along my journey.

A very special thank-you to Ashish, whose patience and technical assistance was invaluable.

I wish to acknowledge my family, and my dear friends for their support and encouragement.

A special expression of gratitude to Kregel Publications, for the privilege of being able to use excerpts from the book, *Number in Scripture*, by E. W. Bullinger;

And, above all, to God be the honor and the glory for evermore.

Thank-you

Part   1

Whoso findeth a wife findeth a good thing, and obtaineth favour of the Lord.

Proverbs 18:22

Chapter 1
What is a Wife?

What is a wife? I have pondered that question over and over again. The answer is so deep that one must consider carefully where to jump in and start swimming in the vast sea of information.

We encounter the very first wife in God's Book of Beginnings; the book of Genesis. Her name was Eve, meaning "mother of all living."

Just as man was created in the image of God, the woman was also created in God's image; "So God created man in His own image, in the image of God created He him; male and female created He them" (Gen. 1:27). Consider the following:

"And the Lord God formed man of the dust of the ground, and breathed into his nostrils the breath of life. Man became a living soul" (Gen. 2:7).

The omnipotent 'I AM'; the God who is from Everlasting to Everlasting; the Alpha and the Omega; the God that created the Heavens and the Earth, and all the host of them; that very same God reached down and put His holy hands in the dust of the ground, and formed a man; His child.

Then I can only imagine that He cupped His precious child's face in His hands, and blew into his nostrils the breath of life. His child became a living soul. These words present such an intimate and personal picture of a God so great and so holy that when Moses insisted on seeing His glory while on top of Mount Sinai, He told Moses that he could only stand to see His glory from behind as He passed by (Ex. 33:18-23). Yet here in the Book of Beginnings, we find God like a sculptor, creating an exquisite object d'art from the *dust,* and making it live with His own breath!

Then, because there was no "help meet" to be found for His precious child, the God of Heaven and Earth caused a deep sleep to come over Adam. While he slept, God removed one of his ribs, and with it, He created a woman.

I find it extremely significant that in addition to naming all of God's creatures, Adam was also given the authority to name his wife. First he called her 'a woman' because she was "taken out of man" (Gen. 2:23), then he called her name 'Eve', for she was "the mother of all living" (Gen. 3:20).

Eve was expressly created by God to be Adam's life partner in the Garden of Eden. She was not only created in the image of God, but she was created from the very flesh of the man himself. She was created to be man's "help meet", his partner and companion. In a profoundly prophetic statement regarding the woman and her purpose, Adam says, "This is now bone of my bones, and flesh of my flesh: she shall be called woman because she was taken out of man. Therefore, shall a man leave his father and his mother, and shall cleave unto *his wife*: and they shall be one flesh" (Gen. 2:23-24).

The second chapter of Genesis closes with the words "And they were both naked, the man and *his wife*, and were not ashamed" (Gen. 2:25).

Just as Jesus told Peter he could have only known that He was the Son of God by enlightenment from the Holy Spirit (Matt. 16:13-17), so I believe that Adam could only have made the statement of Gen. 2:24 through the enlightenment of the Holy Spirit; for as of yet, there was neither father nor mother, and Eve had just arrived on the scene. Nevertheless, this statement establishes from the very foundation of the

3

world as we know it, the purpose and definition of a wife. This statement further prepares us as a church, to understand the purpose and definition of what it means for us to be the Bride of Christ.

In the beginning, a wife was to be man's partner, companion, and helper. She and the man were to keep God's garden, and to be fruitful and multiply. The wife was neither above nor beneath her husband. She was literally taken from a place near to his heart; shielded by the strength of his arm, and of the same flesh as him.

Nevertheless, divine order was apparent when in Gen. 1:26 you find, "And God said, *Let us* ..." It is obvious that God the Father, Son, and Holy Spirit are all represented in this statement, however, God the Father is the one doing the talking. So it is with the man and his wife. The two are one, but the man represents his family.

Everything was fine in the garden until temptation presented itself. As James records in his epistle, temptation led to sin, and sin led to death (James 1:14-15). So it was for Adam and Eve.

Eve's transgression was met with swift judgment from God, for He says to the woman, "I will greatly multiply thy sorrow and thy conception; in sorrow shalt thou bring forth children; and thy desire shall be to thy husband, *and he shall rule over thee*" (Gen.3:16).

*   *   *   *

According to the Scriptures, the wife was created especially by God to be the "help meet" of her husband.

The word *wife* in Hebrew is the same for the word *woman*. It appears that they are interchangeable, suggesting that the woman was created purposely to be a wife.

"And the Lord God said, it is not good that the man should be alone; I will make him an help meet for him."

4

She was made from the very flesh of man himself. Man regains that portion of missing flesh when he takes unto himself a wife. The woman also comes into wholeness otherwise unavailable to her when she is joined together in holy union with the man.

"And the rib, which the Lord God had taken from man, made He a woman, and brought her unto the man.

And Adam said, This is now bone of my bones, and flesh of my flesh: she shall be called Woman, because she was taken out of man.

Therefore shall a man leave his father and his mother, and shall cleave unto his wife: and they shall be one flesh." **Gen. 2:22-24**

This 24th verse of Scripture is so important that it is repeated throughout the New Testament three additional times; twice by Jesus, and once by Paul (Matt.19:5, Mark 10:7, Eph. 5:31).

In Psalm 128, we find that if a man fears God he will be immensely blessed. Not only will he prosper, but the Psalmist writes:

"Thy wife shall be as an fruitful vine by the sides of thine house: thy children like olive plants round about thy table." **Psalm 128:3**

The words of King Solomon regarding a wife tell us a wife is someone that a husband can rejoice with:

"Let thy fountain be blessed: and rejoice with the wife of thy youth." **Prov. 5:18**

She is a good thing to be found, and a man will obtain God's favor by finding a good wife:

"Whoso findeth a wife findeth a good thing, and obtaineth favor of the Lord." **Prov. 18:22**

A contentious (quarrelsome) wife is a perpetual

5

'down':

"A foolish son is the calamity of his father: and the contentions of a wife are a continual dropping."

Prov. 19:13

A prudent wife (one who possesses practical wisdom; one who is judicious and discreet) is from the Lord:

"Houses and riches are the inheritance of the fathers: and a prudent wife is from the Lord."

Prov. 19:14

She is one that her husband is to live joyfully with all the days of his life:

"Live joyfully with the wife whom thou lovest all the days of the life of thy vanity, which He hath given thee under the sun, all the days of thy vanity: for that is thy portion in this life, and in thy labor which thou takest under the sun."
Eccl. 9:9

In the first epistle of Peter we find that a man and his wife are heirs together of the grace of life:

"Likewise, ye husbands, dwell with them (the wife) according to knowledge, giving honor unto the wife as unto the weaker vessel, and as being heirs together of the grace of life; that your prayers be not hindered."
1 Pet. 3:7

In the book of Malachi, chapter 2, verse 14B, a wife is said to be the husband's companion, and covenant partner. These are very strong words, for a covenant is made to be kept and not broken: (Think about how we stand on God's covenants with us - what if God were unreliable, and kept not His word? We'd really be in a mess wouldn't we). The Bible says that we should never vow a vow unto God and not pay it (Eccl. 5:4-5). You need to realize that when you stand at the altar repeating the wedding vows, that in reality the same vow that you make to your spouse, you are making *to* God, and *before* God!

"Yet ye say, Wherefore? Because the Lord hath been witness between thee and the wife of thy youth,

against whom thou hast dealt treacherously: yet is she thy companion, and the wife of thy covenant."

Mal. 2:14

* * * *

The pastor's wife is not always considered in the context of Scripture by the members of the congregation, instead, she is viewed quite differently. I have been in churches where unless you are extremely important, you are not even allowed to occupy the same pew as the pastor's wife, or "First Lady" as we are often called, for she has been exalted.

In other churches the pastor's wife has been blamed for everything from her husband's wrinkled pants, to what his sermon was about on Sunday morning.

I have a friend whose husband is the Pastor of a large, conservative, Presbyterian Church. One day her husband decided that he wanted a pet pig. My friend and I shared quite a few laughs because the congregation loved her husband so much they couldn't believe that such a sweet, loving, conservative fellow could honestly want a pet pig. It had to be his wife's idea!

Many times the members of the congregation want to use the Pastor's wife as their sounding board. They come to complain about the contents of the sermon, the other members of the church, the length of service, why the Pastor didn't run right over to their house when they needed emergency prayer. For some reason that I have yet to understand, certain women seem to be the only ones that have this need. And why does Ms. So and So bring all those kids to church *anyway!*

The Pastor's wife is expected to chair every event and program that exists, and is being thought of, because if the

7

Pastor's wife is involved, it must be righteously important. They want the Pastor's wife to be in their clique, share their gossip, and make sure that she brings her husband to *their* house to eat more often than going to someone else's house. They want the Pastor's wife to analyze their problems, counsel them, and give them advice (that they probably won't take anyway).

Overall, the Pastor's wife is the best friend/greatest obstacle of the members of the congregation. She is the one they want their guests to meet; she is the one they want to have sit at their table during church socials, she is the one whose hairstyle and dress are emulated, evaluated, and criticized, and she is the one that acts as a buffer between her spiritually exhausted husband, and those members of the congregations that would suck his spirit from him like vampires if they could.

　　　　*　　　　*　　　　*　　　　*

Each man has his own personal definition of what *his* wife should be. A godly man is instructed by his Bible to leave his father and mother and cling to his wife. He is further instructed to find pleasure in his *own* wife's breasts; not to withhold himself from her; and to love her as Christ so loved the church that He gave His own life for it (Prov. 5:19, 1 Cor. 7:3-4, Eph. 5:25).

The Bible tells a man that his wife is the one who is to look to his household, and to raise and teach his children.

My husband once told me that he was pleased that I was indeed a godly woman, and set a fine example of what a Pastor's wife should be, *however,* I still needed to realize that he was a man first, and he was a man when he married me, and he had manly desires that needed to be met. (Sometimes we may get a little too holy for our husbands). We are embarrassed if the members of the congregation see us kiss

8

or hold hands.

It is difficult sometimes being a woman, and being a Pastor's wife. There are moments when you want to put on a tantalizing outfit for your husband, and you're absolutely sure that the moment you do, one of the members of your church is going to drop by and say, "hmm, I didn't know that *preachers wives* wore stuff like that!"

I will say to you that being a man's wife is your first responsibility. By committing to marriage, you have made a covenant with that man to be his companion, his lover, and his partner until death do you part.

If you are raising a family, then that becomes your second responsibility. You are responsible for raising the children of the man you married.

Thirdly will come your responsibility to the church. Let me be perfectly clear, your responsibility to the church is not the same as your responsibility to God!

GOD IS ALWAYS FIRST. He comes before your husband, your children, your home, and yourself. This simply means "pray without ceasing," "giving thanks always," and "in all your ways acknowledge Him"(1 Thes.5:17, Eph. 5:20, Prov. 3:6).

I remember one day sitting in BTU (Baptist Training Union) class not too long after I had been going to church. A woman raised her hand, and when the Pastor acknowledged her, this is what she said: "Pastor, I'm having trouble with my husband. He gets upset with me when I go to the hospitals to visit the sick, or I go to visit the shut-ins. *Is he wrong?*" (I have to add here that the way she asked her question, I got the feeling that she visited *a lot*).

The Pastor, a genuinely wizened fellow, asked her the following: "Do you spend time with your husband when he comes home from work? Do you make sure that he has some dinner before you run off to make sure others are being taken care of?"

9

There was quite a pause before the woman looked at him and said "no Pastor."

"In that case, your husband is not wrong to be upset. You must realize that your first duty is to your *own* household."

I have tried to remember that throughout the course of our ministry. Many times you feel like a circus performer trying to juggle a million tasks at once, but always know, your Heavenly Father is there to sustain you and strengthen you, and that nothing is impossible with God (Luke 1:37, 18:27).

As a man, your husband wants a wife. A warm loving body to hold and to be comforted by; an understanding friend who is not going to judge him, or berate him for his shortcomings; someone who will love him unconditionally (when his hair is thinning, when he's getting a little paunchy, when he's moving a little slower). Someone who will make his favorite things to eat, do the things that he likes to do, and let him hold the remote control while you watch TV together.

A Pastor needs a wife who is equally yoked together with him. He needs a wife who is spiritually connected to God so that she will be able to pray him up, watch his back in the Spirit, comfort him when the members of the congregation attempt to exact their pound of flesh, and encourage him to continue in the ministry on those days that he would rather be doing *anything* else.

A Pastor needs a wife who loves him enough to tell him the truth, even when it may not be what he wants to hear.

A Pastor needs a wife who will respect his authority in public. Not that you shouldn't respect your husband all of the time, but we all have moments when we disagree with our spouse. Sometimes we even have difficulty hiding our disgruntlement. Nevertheless, the church is the very last place that you should express your dissatisfaction. It is unprofessional, and unbiblical (1Tim. 3:5, 1Tim. 2:12). As a Pastor's wife, you need to be subject to him the same way that he is to be subject to Jesus Christ.

Finally, as a Pastor's wife, you need to realize that running a church is running a business for God. God is not the author of confusion, and it is disgraceful on our part to forget that thought even for a minute. It is even more disgraceful if we should become the reason for the confusion.

The church should continue in perpetuity until Jesus returns, and we have no right for ANY reason to destroy God's church, and certainly not for our own personal vendettas.

In First Timothy 3:11 we find this description of a (pastor's) and deacon's wife: "Even so must their wives be grave, not slanderers, sober, faithful in all things."

Just as getting married enters you into a covenant agreement with your man, accepting God's call in your life enters you into a covenant agreement with Him. Your personal business should never supersede God's business, and it should never blemish the body of believers that we call the Church.

Chapter 2
The Purpose of a Wife

The word purpose means "to have a fixed design or determination." In the book of Genesis (which is the book of *beginnings*), we find there what God's original purpose was in creating woman.

"And the Lord God said, it is not good that the man should be alone; I will make him an help meet for him." Gen. 2:18

According to Scripture, God created woman to be man's partner in life. As she was formed from the rib, and not from the feet to be beneath, nor the head to be above, I believe that we can safely say that in the beginning, the woman was an equal partner.

"Therefore, shall a man leave his father and his mother, and shall cleave unto his wife: and they shall be one flesh." Gen. 2:24

"For this cause shall a man leave father and mother, and shall cleave to his wife: and they twain shall be one flesh?" Matt. 19:5

"For this cause shall a man leave his father and mother, and cleave to his wife;

And they twain shall be one flesh: so then they are no more twain, but one flesh.

What therefore God hath joined together, let not man put asunder." Mark 10:7-9

"For this cause shall a man leave his father and mother, and shall be joined unto his wife, and they two shall be one flesh." Eph. 5:31

Practically speaking:

"Two are better than one; because they have a good reward for their labor.

For if they fall, the one will lift up his fellow: but woe to him that is alone when he falleth; for he hath not another to help him up." Prov. 4:9-10

As a result of her transgression, not only was the woman punished, but the Bible says, "the whole creation groaneth and travaileth in pain together until now" (Romans 8:22). We really have no idea what life would have been like, or could have been like, had the woman not been the transgressor.

As a result of Eve's transgression, EVERYTHING was cursed, and will remain that way until Jesus returns.

"Unto the woman He said, I will greatly multiply thy sorrow and thy conception; in sorrow shalt thou bring forth children; and thy desire shall be to thy husband, and he shall rule over thee." Gen. 3:16

This one little tiny piece of Scripture has changed woman's place in the world forever!

Obligations and Duties

To your husband:

"Thou shalt not commit adultery." Ex. 20:14

"And if a woman shall put away her husband, and be married to another, she committeth adultery." Mark 10:12

"For the woman which hath an husband is bound by the law to her husband so long as he liveth; but if the husband be dead, she is loosed from the law of her husband.

So then if, while her husband liveth, she be married to another man, she shall be called an adulteress: but if her husband be dead, she is free from the law; so that she is no adulteress, though she be married to another man."   Rom. 7:2-3

"Nevertheless, to avoid fornication, let every man have his own wife, and let every woman have her own husband.

Let the husband render unto the wife due benevolence: and likewise also the wife unto the husband.

The wife hath not power of her own body, but the husband: and likewise also the husband hath not power of his own body, but the wife.

Defraud ye not one the other, except it be with consent for a time, that ye may give yourselves to fasting and prayer; and come together again, that Satan tempt you not for your incontinency."   1 Cor. 7:2-5

"And unto the married, I command, yet not I, but the Lord, Let not the wife depart from her husband:

But and if she depart, let her remain unmarried, or be reconciled to her husband: and let not the husband put away his wife."   1 Cor. 7:10-11

"Wives, submit yourselves unto your own husbands, as unto the Lord.

Therefore, as the church is subject unto Christ, so let the wives be to their own husbands in every thing."
Eph. 5:22,24

14

Somehow society has promoted the concept that women are subject to *all* men. As you can clearly see here, that concept is not true. Wives are subject to THEIR OWN HUSBANDS, no one else's.

To your Pastor/husband:

"Let your women keep silence in the churches: for it is not permitted unto them to speak; but they are commanded to be under obedience, as also saith the law.

And if they will learn anything, let them ask their husbands at home: for it is a shame for women to speak in the church."   1 Cor. 14:34-35

"But every woman that prayeth or prophesieth with her head uncovered, dishonoreth her head: for that is even all one as if she were shaven."   1 Cor. 11:5

"Wives, submit yourselves unto your own husbands, as unto the Lord.

For the husband is the head of the wife, even as Christ is the head of the church: and He is the saviour of the body.

Therefore, as the church is subject unto Christ, so let the wives be to their own husbands in every thing.

Husbands, love your wives, even as Christ also loved the church, and gave Himself for it;

That He might sanctify and cleanse it with the washing of water by the word,

That He might present it to Himself a glorious church, not having spot, or wrinkle, or any such thing; but that it should be holy and without blemish.

So ought men to love their wives as their own bodies. He that loveth his wife loveth himself.

For no man ever yet hated his own flesh; but

15

nourisheth and cherisheth it, even as the Lord the church:

For we are members of His body, of His flesh, and of His bones.

For this cause shall a man leave his father and mother, and shall be joined unto his wife, and they two shall be one flesh.

This is a great mystery: but I speak concerning Christ and the church.

Nevertheless let every one of you in particular so love his wife even as himself; and the wife see that she reverence her husband."   Eph. 5:22-33

"In like manner also, that women adorn themselves in modest apparel, with shamefacedness and sobriety; not with broided hair, or gold, or pearls, or costly array;

But which becometh women professing godliness with good works.

Let the woman learn in silence with all subjection.

But I suffer not a woman to teach, nor usurp the authority over the man, but to be in silence.

For Adam was first formed, then Eve.

<u>And Adam was not deceived, but the woman being deceived was in the transgression</u>. (emphasis mine)

Notwithstanding she shall be saved in childbearing, if they continue in faith and charity and holiness with sobriety."   1 Tim. 2:9-15

"Even so must their wives be grave, not slanderers, sober, faithful in all things."
1 Tim. 3:11

"The aged women likewise, that they be in behavior as becometh holiness, not false accusers, not given to much wine, teachers of good things;

That they may teach the young women to be sober, to love their husbands, to love their children,

To be discreet, chaste, keepers at home, good, obedient to their own husbands, that the word of God be not blasphemed." Titus 2:3-5

To your children:

"My son, keep thy father's commandment, and forsake not <u>the law of thy mother</u>. (emphasis mine)

Bind them continually upon thine heart, and tie them about thy neck.

When thou goest, it shall lead thee; when thou sleepest, it shall keep thee; and when thou awakest, it shall talk with thee.

For the commandment is a lamp; and the law is light; and reproofs of instruction are the way of life." Prov. 6:20-23

"A wise son maketh a glad father: but a foolish son is the heaviness of his mother." Prov. 10:1

"Even a child is known by his doings, whether his work be pure, and whether it be right." Prov. 20:11

Your position in the scheme of things

"A virtuous woman is a crown to her husband: but she that maketh ashamed is as rottenness in his bones." Prov. 12:4

"But I would have you know, that the head of every man is Christ; and the head of the woman is the man; and the head of Christ is God." 1 Cor. 11:3

"For a man indeed ought not to cover *his* head, forasmuch *as* he is the image and the glory of God: but the woman is the glory of the man.

For the man is not of the woman; but the woman of the man.

Neither was the man created for the woman; but the woman for the man.

For this cause ought the woman have power on *her* head because of the angels.

Nevertheless neither is the man without the woman, neither the woman without the man, in the Lord.

For as the woman *is* of the man, even so *is* the man also by the woman; but all things of God."

1 Cor. 11:7-12

Chapter 3
Examples of Godly Wives

The wives in this chapter as well as chapter five, are listed in the order we encounter them in the Bible. They have been divided into two separate categories; godly or un-godly, the exception being chapter four, which is the chapter about Eve. Eve was created in the image of God, but she was beguiled by the serpent, and transgressed the laws of God, and in the end she was as one of us; a repentant sinner.

A short synopsis of their attributes or lack thereof, together with Scripture references will be followed with an assessment of how their lives affected the lives of those around them.

People have the tendency to think that what they do is their own business. I'm here to tell you that this statement is absolutely untrue! No matter how much we don't want to hear it, how we live affects both people we know, and people we don't know.

Mrs. Noah:
Genesis chapter 6 vs.18, chapter 7 vs. 7,13, chapter 8 vs. 16,18

We encounter Mrs. Noah beginning in the sixth chapter of Genesis. She is mentioned five times between chapters six and eight, never by name, only as Noah's wife.

However, if we take the time to scrutinize the account of Noah and his undertaking of God's commandment to him, we must realize that without Mrs. Noah, her husband might not have been able to do his job.

We find Noah, whom the Bible says is a just man,

perfect in his generations, and one who walks with God, living on the plains with his family, in the midst of sin so gross, that God has repented of ever making man (Gen. 6:6,9).

Since the creation there has been no rain; yet God tells Noah the he must build an Ark and fill it with two of every kind of living thing for it shall rain forty days and forty nights, and the world will be destroyed (Gen. 7:4).

It took Noah 120 years to complete the Ark. During that time, he was ridiculed, scorned, and laughed at.

Can you imagine being Noah's wife!

Your husband comes in from prayer one day and tells you that God has just told him to build a huge ship and fill it with two of every living thing, because God will be sending a flood with waters so great that the entire world will be covered with water, and every living thing not aboard the Ark will perish.

Because God desires to save not only Noah, but his entire household as well, we can safely say that unlike the vapid, and indifferent Mrs. Noah recently portrayed in the television version of Noah's Ark, the Biblical Mrs. Noah more than likely shared her husband's dedication, understanding, and trust of the God they both worshiped, and served; and instructed their sons in the same.

Furthermore, it goes without question that in order for her husband and sons to build continually on the Ark, they would need to be fed, their clothes would have needed mending, they would have needed hot baths, and probably some occasional first aid.

I can picture Mrs. Noah not only taking diligent care of her husband, but instructing the wives of her sons in their duties as well.

As the matriarch of the family, it would have been Mrs. Noah's job to handle the gathering, preparation, and storing of the food and other supplies needed for her family, and the animals. (No small task.)

20

I'm sure that every day when Noah finished his work, he was not only tired, but also discouraged. Can you imagine preaching to people every day for 120 years, and not seeing one contrite or penitent spirit ever? Worse yet had to be the realization that these same unrepentant people, because of the hardness of their hearts, would soon be destroyed.

And finally, Mrs. Noah spent approximately one year and seventeen days cooped up in that boat with her family and all of those animals (Gen. 7:10-12,17,24, Gen. 8:3-6,10,12-14, Halley's Bible Handbook, pg. 74).

Again, unlike the atrocious movie portrayal, we do not find Mrs. Noah going stir crazy and painting herself up like some kind of pagan, but rather we find peace and patience resting upon the Ark and all of its inhabitants.

All in all, I would say that Mrs. Noah was quite a remarkable woman. A faithful, encouraging, and supportive wife; a patient and trusting servant of God; a mother diligent in her duties and responsibilities as the matriarch of her family, and not unlike that unnamed women of Proverbs 31.

The unnamed woman of Proverbs 31:
Proverbs 31:1,10-31

This woman has been both my fascination and my obsession since having encountered her in one of my daily Bible readings.

I would be terribly remiss if I did not begin here by commending the mother of King Lemuel;(believed to be the king of Massa). There are some theological questions raised as to exactly who this king is, but for our purposes, it really doesn't matter. We are interested only in the sound and timeless advice given to him by his unnamed mother. God bless her!

I remember the first time that I read this Scripture, I cried and cried. Never had I seen myself so far from the mark of spiritual and womanly perfection. I was sure in my heart that I could never be her. However, I'm glad to tell you that all things are possible with God, and I become more and more like her every day.

"Who can find a virtuous woman? For her price is far above rubies.

The heart of her husband doth safely trust in her, so that he shall have no need of spoil.

She will do him good and not evil all the days of her life.

She seeketh wool, and flax, and worketh willingly with her hands.

She is like the merchant's ships; she bringeth her food from afar.

She riseth also while it is yet night, and giveth meat to her household, and a portion to her maidens.

She considereth a field, and buyeth it: with the fruit of her hands she planteth a vineyard.

She girdeth her loins with strength, and strengtheneth her arms.

She perceiveth that her merchandise is good: her candle goeth not out by night.

She layeth her hands to the spindle, and her hands hold the distaff.

She stretcheth out her hand to the poor; yea she reacheth forth her hands to the needy.

She is not afraid of the snow for her household are clothed with scarlet.

She maketh herself coverings of tapestry; her clothing is silk and purple.

Her husband is known in the gates, when he sitteth among the elders of the land.

She maketh fine linen, and selleth it; and delivereth girdles unto the merchant.

Strength and honor are her clothing; and she shall rejoice in time to come.

She openeth her mouth with wisdom; and in her tongue is the law of kindness.

She looketh well to the ways of her household, and eateth not the bread of idleness.

Her children arise up and call her blessed; her husband also, and he praiseth her.

Many daughters have done virtuously, but thou excellest them all.

Favor is deceitful, and beauty is vain: but a woman that feareth the Lord, she shall be praised.

Give her of the fruit of her hands; and let her own works praise her in the gates."

Prov. 31:10-31

There is really very little to add here. I will say to you, set your aspirations very high.

Since the sixties and seventies, the media has "blitzed" women with the feminist idea of successful womanhood in a effort to encourage women into moving away from being the type of woman that is presented here. Instead of aspiring to be an excellent housekeeper, wife and mother, it is implied that this concept is beneath us. Instead, we are beguiled, coaxed, and cajoled into striving for equity in the workplace, in our sexual relationships, in the bawdy way that we present ourselves in public, and in our sin.

In the seventies, I remember how the media portrayed the "stay at home" mothers, and the homemakers as women whose lives were lacking excitement and adventure; women who were not in control of their own destinies, being subject to their husbands. In retrospect, I have to laugh because now the media's female role models are single women going from relationship to relationship, or women raising families alone. I thank God for the women who continued to remain homemakers, and stay at home mothers, even when it seemed old fashioned.

When we went to school, we were never told to aspire to be a good wife, mother, or housekeeper. Rather, we were told to fight and claw our way to the top of the world's idea of success in (male) society, and that anything less than corporate success made us a failure.

As a result, so many of us have missed out on the greatest blessings and treasures a corrupt and cursed world had to offer. Upon receiving salvation, many tried to regain these personal relationships with children and husbands, while others who were not so fortunate could only grieve for having misguided priorities.

In the last few years, violent acts committed by children have reached an epidemic proportion. When the incident occurred at the Columbine High School in Colorado, the front page of our local newspaper said, "WHY?"
I thought to myself, "why not . . . what do you expect!?"

Children are left to raise themselves; there is no longer a definitive line between right and wrong, and 'mommy' is too busy trying to get her own needs met to have time to meet the needs of others. If you wonder why I say 'mommy' and not 'daddy', it is because it is the husband's job to provide, and the wife's job to raise and nurture.

Because I am writing in the 21st Century instead of the 18th Century, I am confronted with the overwhelming urge to apologize for speaking the truth; however, praise God, I remain an overcomer! If you wonder why I have to regress as far as the 18th Century, it's because by the 19th Century the fight was already on for women's equity. I am all for the vote, equal pay for equal work, and better health care for women. However, of the three things named, we as women have only achieved one. What we did get was birth control so we could "love 'em and leave 'em, "no fault" divorce, and a plethora of communicable diseases (most of which are incurable).

I do work myself, but my job does not come before my family. I still do laundry and homework; I still cook dinner and iron clothes; I still spend every available minute being a constructive part of the lives of my family, and in the training and nurturing of my children.

God really can make all things possible for you that your life might be lived to His glory; but *you* must have the desire for righteousness. You don't need to try and make yourself righteous, because you can't! Just have the desire to be what God wants you to be; even if you think you won't like it; by the time you become it, you'll like it and be satisfied with it as well; (trust me).

Hannah:
1 Samuel 1:2-28, 2:1-21

I believe Hannah is probably one of my most favorite women in the Bible.

We meet her in the opening verses of the first book of Samuel; one of two wives. Albeit she is the wife most beloved by her husband, (1 Sam. 1:5,8) she is childless, and continually tormented by her husband's other wife (1 Sam. 1:2, 6-7); all in all, a rather dysfunctional family atmosphere.

Nevertheless, we find Hannah faithfully worshiping and making the yearly pilgrimage to sacrifice at the temple at Shiloh, as was the custom of her day.

What I admire most about Hannah, is that she was subject to her husband as the Bible says we should be. Never do we find scriptural evidence that she confronts her husband about the way she is treated by his other wife, nor is she bitter or angry towards him because of her barrenness.

I imagine that she was a loving and tender wife, for the Bible says that her husband loved her very much, and it is obvious that he was sensitive to her condition, possibly being more attentive to her because of it (1 Sam. 1:5, 8). Yet

Hannah had boldness before the Lord, for she dared even to make a covenant with Him.

Many times we want something from God, but we are hesitant to give up something in return, let alone sacrifice that thing He has given us that His glory might be evident in His gift to us.

Hannah prayed for a son and made a vow unto God for him:

"Oh Lord of hosts, if thou wilt indeed look on the affliction of thine handmaid, and remember me, and not forget thine handmaid, but wilt give unto thine handmaid a man child, then I will give him unto the Lord all the days of his life, and there shall no razor come upon his head"(1 Sam. 1:11).

In the last phrase of this prayer, Hannah vows to consecrate her unborn son to the service of the Lord. His uncut hair would serve as a sign, but unlike the regular Nazarite priests who serve for a prescribed time, Hannah commits her son to a lifetime of service. This she does three times (1 Sam. 1:11, 22, 28). Three is a very significant number. (Please reference Appendix B for additional information concerning numbers in scripture.)

So fervent was her un-uttered prayer that Eli the priest thought she was drunk.

Then Eli, realizing his mistake and her piety, comforts her with the following words, "Go in peace: and the God of Israel grant thee thy petition that thou hast asked of Him" (1 Sam. 1:17).

The Bible goes on to say that Hannah went her way, "and her countenance was no more sad" (verse 18). Hannah had faith. She believed that God not only heard her prayer, but that He would also answer her prayer. As a matter of fact, she wastes no time, because as soon as she got back home, the Bible says, "Elkannah knew Hannah his wife; and the Lord remembered her" (verse 19).

There is much depth in Hannah's story. For she

conceives and names her son Samuel which means "asked of the Lord." She tends and nurtures her little boy in preparation for the fulfillment of her vow to God. At the appointed time, after he has been weaned, the family travels to the temple at Shiloh to worship, and to leave little Samuel as she had promised.

"But Hannah went not up; for she said unto her husband, I will not go up until the child be weaned, and then I will bring him, that he may appear before the Lord, and there abide *for ever*" (1 Sam. 1:22).

She is not selfish like many of us. *Forever* is an awfully long time. Nevertheless, we do not find her working her wiles on her husband that he with their whole family might move to Shiloh where she can be near her little son, but rather we find her keeping her home, raising additional children, and making the yearly pilgrimage to Shiloh to worship, and to bring her son a new coat made with her own hands.

I would be remiss if I concluded this section on Hannah without mentioning what the scholars call *Hannah's Song*. There have been a number of things written about the song of Hannah; some scholars believe that Hannah's song encouraged Mary's Magnificat in the New Testament. Hannah's song has its own special meaning for me.

In the first year of my Salvation, I was overwhelmed with the word of God. What I mean is, every time I read the Bible, it seemed that God was speaking directly to me. I can remember sitting in the choir loft, opening my Bible because the preacher was getting ready to preach. On this particular Sunday, which happened to be Mother's Day, he was going to preach from the first chapter of the First Book of Samuel. I cannot remember the particular portion of Scripture that he spoke from, but it ended way before Hannah's song. Nevertheless, I was compelled to read further. As he preached, I'm sorry to say, I continued reading; I couldn't help myself... This is what I read.

27

"And Hannah prayed, and said, My heart rejoiceth in the Lord, mine horn is exalted in the Lord: my mouth is enlarged over mine enemies: because I rejoice in thy salvation."   1 Sam. 2:1

I wasn't exactly sure what that meant, but we had recently been homeless and displaced, and now we were not. I was at peace with myself because God had given me peace so I didn't feel that we had any enemies (which was foolish on my part), but this verse assured me that my enemies, if I had any, were being taken care of by the Lord. And my heart was continually rejoicing in the salvation of God.

"There is none holy as the Lord: for there is none beside thee: neither is there any rock like our God."
1 Sam. 2:2

Being an avid reader, I marveled at beauty and the liquidity of the words used by this woman to describe a God that she obviously knew intimately; a God that I was just getting to know. I hoped in my heart that when I worshiped and praised God that such beautiful words would also flow from my tongue and sound as beautiful to Him as I was sure these words from Hannah sounded. I also wanted to be as secure in my faith as Hannah was.

"Talk no more so exceeding proudly; let not arrogancy come out of your mouth: for the Lord is a God of knowledge, and by him actions are weighed."
1 Sam. 2:3

This verse made me fearful of God because I was arrogant and I had been proud as well. The fact that God would weigh my actions made me a little concerned to say the least. I decided to consider all of my future actions very carefully before I did anything rash.

"The bows of the mighty men are broken, and they that stumble are girded with strength."   1 Sam. 2:4

I was not familiar with the verse that said, " ...my (God's) strength is made perfect in weakness" (2 Cor. 12:9). However I did understand that our own physical strength was

28

meaningless. This verse made me consider how we used to be; those times in our lives that we lived by might and intimidation, and made our way according to our will.

"They that were full have hired out themselves for bread; and they that were hungry ceased: so that the barren hath born seven; and she that hath many children is waxed feeble." 1 Sam. 2:5

I had no idea what this meant, and quite honestly I kind of breezed over it. Revisiting this verse, three things come to mind. The first is that people develop a false security when everything seems to be going their way; they have substantial funds set back for their retirement; there is more than enough food in the pantry; they've never been sick a day in their life, nevertheless, things happen and we find the rug of security pulled out from under us. "They that were full have hired out themselves for bread." Truthfully, our securities are false, and we find ourselves depending on the things created and not the Creator. God's security is true, and everlasting. It will not be digested to leave us hungry again; it can never be used up or mismanaged like social security; it will never wane or wax dull. God alone is able to feed the hungry (literally and figuratively) so that "they that *were* hungry ceased."

The second thing that I see in this verse is that Hannah is speaking of herself, in addition to praising God on behalf of all barren women who had been blessed with child as she had, when she says, "the barren hath born seven." Not that she had born seven herself, for the Bible says that Hannah had in addition to Samuel "three sons and two daughters" (1 Sam. 2:21).

I believe this to be a figurative number, and not a literal number. There is great significance in the number seven, for seven denotes spiritual perfection.

And lastly, I believe that Hannah is speaking directly about Peninnah and others like her when she says "she that hath many children is waxed feeble."

We meet Peninnah in verse two of the first chapter of the First Book of Samuel. The Bible says she "had children." In verse four we find Elkhannah giving to the wives their portion to sacrifice, and "he gave to Peninnah his wife, and to *all* her sons and her daughters, portions": The fact that her children are not numbered in verse two, coupled with the word "all" in verse four, implies that Peninnah had *many* children.

We further find Peninnah instead of being grateful to God for His blessing of many children, spending her energy "provoking her adversary (Hannah) sore, for to make her fret, because the Lord had shut up her womb" (verse 6).

Lastly we find that Peninnah is not satisfied with simply provoking Hannah occasionally, but rather her provocation is continual, for we read, "as he did so year by year, when she went up to the house of the Lord, so she provoked her" . . . (verse 7).

So as God continued to keep Hannah's womb shut, Peninnah continued to provoke Hannah, and gain pleasure from her pain.

There are so many women out there that have children for the wrong reason. Maybe it's just me, but I feel that Peninnah is one of these women. I have not read in Scripture that she took pleasure in any of her children, or that she loved them, or even that her husband had pleasure with them. It seems that they were simply a means to elevate her above her rival; instruments of pain with which she could afflict poor Hannah, and security to make sure that her husband kept her, (both physically and materially).

After verse seven, Peninnah is surgically removed from the pages of Scripture never to be mentioned again; neither she, nor her children.

I had the occasion some time ago, to speak to a modern day Peninnah. She was sharing with me her life's miseries; I listened to her attentively, and even though my flesh did not want to sympathize with her, my spirit could not help it.

You see, I *knew* this Peninnah very well. Fourteen years ago her husband came home to find her pregnant with another man's child.

She has used her children for so many years, that they have grown up to be users themselves. They regard neither God nor man; god is simply a word that comes before damn, and man is someone that they need to take advantage of before he takes advantage of them.

As she related to me how the daughters ran and still run away from home; sneak out of their house; have sex, drink, smoke and take drugs, and threaten her with bodily harm if she tries to administer discipline, and how the son, (the lesser of the evils) is lazy with a very poor attitude, and a Peter Pan complex, my heart began to ache for her.

We are about three years different in age, and yet she appears to be at least twenty years older than I am. Her body is beginning to fail her, and she is presently unable to hold any type of job for very long. "She that hath many children is waxed feeble." She is old before her time; her body is breaking down, and she is used up.

Truly her children reflect her. They are doing everything that she did and does. I am sad that they were not important enough to her to nurture, but were simply little insurance policies. I am sorry for her. There is no amount of money in the world to compensate for children that have no regard for you. They would just as soon kill you in your sleep as kiss you on the cheek.

Peninnah wasted her time and her life and her children using them as tools against Hannah, for Hannah (looking neither to the left nor the right as Mother Steward used to say) simply focused on God, and her life was blessed. Not only was her life blessed, the entire Nation of Israel, and we as readers of the Scriptures have been blessed by the life of Samuel.

31

"The Lord killeth, and maketh alive: he bringeth down to the grave, and bringeth up.

The Lord maketh poor, and maketh rich: he bringeth low, and lifteth up.

He raiseth up the poor out of the dust, and lifteth up the beggar from the dunghill, to set them among princes, and to make them inherit the throne of glory: for the pillars of the earth are the Lord's, and he hath set the world upon them."
1 Sam. 2:6-8

I remember underlining this section as I sat in the church that day reading. I was made to realize that ALL THINGS were in God's power to do with as He wished. I also realized that no one had control over their own fate, or another's. People elevate themselves so high never understanding that God has lifted them up, and God can bring them down.

These verses spoke to me of God's awesome power, and my own insignificance in the scheme of things.

These verses comforted me as I sat on my own dunghill; a poor beggar, because they made me to know that I was heir to an inheritance far greater than any wealth that could ever be accumulated or inherited in a lifetime. And in the meantime, by no power of our own, God has caused my husband and I to be able to 'walk among princes'.

"He will keep the feet of his saints, and the wicked shall be silent in darkness; for by strength shall no man prevail."
1 Sam. 2:9

I had often wondered about wicked people, and sometimes I still do, for many of them profess to be Christians. I wondered if God would let them into Heaven simply because they confessed a belief in Jesus as their Savior.

I also wondered, being a new Christian, if I would be able to stay on that narrow road, and not slip off. This verse assured me that God was capable of keeping me. I was relieved.

And lastly, I wondered about Christians who were quick to say "God's will be done," but as soon as God's will was not their will, they would fly off the handle, push their weight around, back bite and back stab, to get their will accomplished. In other words, they would try to prevail by strength. I was grateful to know that no man would prevail by strength against the will of God.

"The adversaries of the Lord shall be broken to pieces; out of heaven shall he thunder upon them: the Lord shall judge the ends of the earth; and he shall give strength unto his king, and exalt the horn of his anointed." 1 Sam. 2:10

This is clearly a Messianic prophecy, which speaks of the eminent and anticipated return of our Lord and Savior, Jesus Christ in that great day of the Lord.

Priscilla:
Acts 18:2,18,26   Romans 16:3   1 Corinthians 16:19   2 Timothy 4:19

As I began the research for this portion concerning Aquila, and his wife Priscilla, I ran into some conflicting statements. The female writers tend to put Priscilla first above her husband citing that her name appears first more times in the Bible than his, therefore, she must be more learned and righteous than he. They also write that Priscilla expounded to Apollos, and that Priscilla had established a church in *her* home. Unfortunately for the feminist Christians, this is not true. The Bible says, "God is not the author of confusion . . ." (1 Cor. 14:33).

If you look up the Scriptures that talk about Priscilla and her husband, you will find their names listed in this manner: "Aquila . . . with his wife, Priscilla" (Acts 18:2), "Priscilla and Aquila" (Acts 18:18), "Aquila and Priscilla" (Acts 18:26), "Priscilla and Aquila" (Rom. 16:3), "Aquila and

Priscilla" (1 Cor. 16:3), "...Prisca and Aquila" (2 Tim. 4:19). As you can see, each is listed first three times; one does not come first more times than the other.

The reason for the inclusion of Priscilla in the list of godly wives, is because Priscilla and her husband fulfill the godly standard of the man and his wife being one flesh, and set an eternal example of how we are to live with our husbands.

Priscilla and her husband were one in many ways. They were one in marital bliss, for one is never mentioned without the other. The Bible says that Paul "found a certain Jew named Aquila, with his wife, Priscilla."

The Bible also shows us that Priscilla and her husband were one in their secular occupation.

The Bible infers that when Paul met this couple, they were already established in the Christian faith. Priscilla and her husband were one in their Christian service, as well as their knowledge of the Scriptures.

We get a vivid picture of the couple as humble and gentle servants of Christ. A couple whose interest was not in elevating themselves, but rather, serving in whatever capacity the Lord saw fit. We get a glimpse into their humble character when they meet Apollos, whom the Bible says is a learned and eloquent man from Alexandria, who has come to preach in the church at Ephesus. The Bible says that he was learned in the way of John the Baptist, but he did not know the Gospel of Jesus Christ. The Bible goes on to say that "when Aquila and Priscilla had heard, they took him unto *them*, and expounded unto him the way of God more perfectly" (Acts 18:26).

This is something that they obviously did together, and it was not for self-edification, but for the edification of the Saints. The Bible shows us that Apollos went on to become a great preacher of the faith, which he couldn't have done had he not met Priscilla and her husband.

34

The fact that "they took him unto them" shows that they opened their home to Apollos and spent time with him, teaching him in Christian love those things that he would need to be the preacher that God called him to be.

They also had a church in their home. No mean feat in those days when Christians were openly persecuted for Christ's sake. This undertaking had to be done by mutual consent.

Lastly I will end with these verses from Paul (Rom. 16:3-4), "Greet Priscilla and Aquila my helpers in Christ Jesus:

Who have for my life laid down their own necks: unto whom not only I give thanks, but also all the churches of the Gentiles."

Whatever it was that caused them to put their lives on the line for Paul was a blessing not only to the disciple, but to the entire Gentile church as well.

Overall, I feel that Priscilla shows us what a godly wife could be, and should be. She shows us that it is possible to be together with your husband in all things including God's service. And most of all, she shows how much can be done by two who act as one. If we reflect on the results of the life lived by Priscilla and her husband, we see the monumental effect they had on the entire Church; not only in their day, but in ours as well.

Strive for godly unity with your husband. Let his agenda be your agenda, and the service you do for God be unanimous.

When you stand before the throne of God and He judges you according to those things done in your body, let Him be able to address both of you at once if it is His desire; and truly, as He addresses both of you at once, pray that He could also address you in the midst of the entire body, which is the body of Christ.

Chapter 4
EVE
Genesis chapters 2-3, 4:1-2,25, 5:2-4   2 Corinthians 11:3, 1 Timothy 2:13

Eve is probably the most complex of all the women in the Bible. So much so that I have given her a chapter unto herself.

She begins godly enough, being created in the image of God Himself; that is to say, a three part being with a spirit, a soul, and a body. She then finds herself an ungodly woman, and the reason for the world being cast into the abyss of sin until the return of Christ. Finally, she finds herself in the position of repentant sinner.

As one begins to dissect Eve; her character and her situation, it is like peeling a huge onion. The more you peel, the more it becomes evident that there are more layers yet to come.

Eve was the 'first' in many categories. She was the first and only woman ever created by God. She must have been exquisite; perfect in every way; intellectually, physically, and spiritually (Gen. 1:26-27, 2:22-23).

She was the only woman never to be born in sin, for she was created, and without sin (Gen. 5:2).

She was the first woman to ever try to fool God by covering herself with her own righteousness instead of God's righteousness (Gen. 3:7).

She was the first liar (Gen. 2:17, 3:3), which is simple enough to say, but what happened was a little more complex than that, and we should take care when we are tempted to do the same thing. Bullinger calls it "the three-fold corruption of God's Word."

By taking from,
   adding to, and
   altering.
This led up to the *first* sin.

(1) God had said, "of every tree in the garden thou mayest FREELY eat" (Gen. 2:16). In repeating this, Eve *omitted* the word "freely" (3:2) making God less bountiful than He was.

(2) God had said, "But of the tree of the Knowledge of Good and Evil, thou shalt not eat of it" (Gen. 2:17). In repeating this Eve *added* the words, "NEITHER SHALL YE TOUCH IT" (Gen. 3:3) making God more severe than He was.

(3) God has said, "Thou shalt SURELY die" (Gen. 3:17). In repeating this Eve *altered* it to, "Lest ye die" (Gen. 3:3) thus weakening the certainty of the Divine threat into a contingency.

E.W. Bullinger, Number in Scripture, Kregel Publications, pgs. 116,117

She was the first wife, and the first mother, and grandmother (Gen. 2:23-24, 3:20, 4:1-2, 17, 25-26).

She was the first woman to ever experience 'spiritual' death, (separation from God), and the first mother to ever lose a child to physical death (Gen. 3:24, 4:8).

She was the first mother to ever have a child who committed a violent act (Gen. 4:8).

She was the first woman to ever be assailed by the Devil, and the first to sin (Gen. 3:1-7).

She was the first person to see the results of her sin, and it's effect (Gen. 3:14-19, Rom. 8:22).

She witnessed the first sacrificial shedding of blood for man (kind's) sin (Gen. 3:21).

She was the first woman to hear the first of God's messianic prophecies (Gen. 3:15).

*   *   *   *

Food for Thought:

Eve was the first woman to come in contact with

Satan's "Four Spiritual Lies" as Dr. Maurice Rawlings calls them. These four lies form the basis of much of what is being preached in the New Age religions that are bombarding us in this age before the coming of Christ. In his book, *To Hell and Back*, Dr. Rawlings makes the following observation:

> The four lies, Satan's unchanging promises, are so compacted that the depth of their meaning escapes casual inspection.
> But the serpent said to the woman [1] "You will not die. For God knows that when you eat of it [2] your eyes will be opened, and [3] you will be like God, [4] knowing good and evil." (RSV).
> Dr. Maurice Rawlings, To Hell and Back, Thomas Nelson Publishers, pg. 161

The first lie that Eve believed was, "Ye shall not surely die:" (Gen. 3:4). It didn't seem to matter that God has specifically said that "...of the tree of the knowledge of good and evil, thou shalt not eat of it: for in that day thou shalt surely die" (Gen. 2:17). This ancient lie has proved to be the basis for a universal, and ecumenical belief in reincarnation; simply meaning, to die and live again.

The most familiar definition of reincarnation is the belief that after one dies, they will return again, and again, and again, evolving up or down depending on the previous lives they lived, until they have perfected life; finally dying, and becoming one with the Universe.

However, the devil is a subtle creature; the Bible says that he sometimes appears as an "angel of light" (2 Cor. 11:14). The New Age has successfully incorporated the old with the new. Everyone may not agree that a person can die again, again, and again, but there are many who consult the mediums to glean advice from dead relatives *living* in the hereafter. There is the belief that since we are matter, we simply return to matter, and become a larger part of the matter of the universe, ergo, continuing to live in a different form. The movie The Lion King, informed us that we were all simply a part of the "great circle of life", kind of like re-cycling, first you were a cardboard box, and now you're a greeting card. All of these are forms of reincarnation.

The Bible clearly tells us that, "... it is appointed unto men once to die, but after this the judgment" (Heb. 9:27).

Once Eve ate of the fruit, her "eyes would be opened" (Gen. 3:15). Satan implied that by disobeying God, Eve would have access to knowledge heretofore unavailable to her: *hidden knowledge*. Dr. Rawlings calls this the "basis of Esotericism" (Ibid, page 161).

Esotericism is defined as a pursuit and practice of hidden knowledge. Since ancient times, Satan has fanned the flames of humanity's desire for hidden knowledge. Evidence of this can be found throughout history in the archaeological discoveries of secret cults and societies.

I have on my bookshelf various publications from purveyors of hidden knowledge that I have collected over the years. I use them from time to time when I have the opportunity to speak on New Age doctrines, and how they have infiltrated our lives and our churches.

Some modern day Esoterics would include those who belong to Masonic or other similar secret organizations, modern day Druids, covens of witches, those who are privy to information supplied by their spirit guides, and those practicing a variety of Eastern Arts, like yoga, and martial arts.

Satan further suggested to Eve that by eating of the fruit of the tree of the knowledge of good and evil, she would "be as gods" (Gen. 3:5). Dr. Rawlings calls this the "basis of Pantheism" (Ibid, page 162).

Pantheism is the belief that man and matter, God and the Universe are one. In other words, everything is a part of God, and God is a part of everything.

The New Age has extended this idea to the point where people are not satisfied with being a part of God, it is their desire to *become* God. Unfortunately, there are enough people out there who are more than willing to help you find the god within yourself.

Satan's reasoning behind telling Eve if she ate of the tree she would be as god, was because she "would know good and evil" (Gen. 3:5).

No more would she have to depend on God to tell her what was good and what was evil, she would be able to tell herself. This knowledge has allowed mankind to decide for themselves what is good and what is evil. Dr. Rawlings calls this the "basis of Relativism" (Ibid, page 162).

The basic idea of Relativism is that a thing is *relative* according to its relation to something else. In other words, an action is assessed in accordance to its position in regards to a particular situation.

People should be able to, and those who are *enlightened* certainly can, make their own decisions as to what is good and what is evil.

Everywhere around us we are assaulted with this "doctrine of devils" (1 Tim. 4:1). Abortion is not murder, but it is "pro-choice." Homosexuality is not an "abomination", it is simply an alternative lifestyle, witchcraft is not necessarily evil, for one can be a "white witch" using their craft for good. Sex may not necessarily be sex anymore; it now depends on what your definition of sex is.

The Bible tells us that there are those who would "call evil good, and good evil" (Is. 5:20). We live in an age where this attitude seems to be commonplace. Judge for yourselves if indeed mankind possesses the ability to know good from evil.

I have included this information in this chapter concerning Eve because just like Eve, we still question God and make decisions that exclude him. Just like Eve, we desire to have hidden knowledge, and to be elevated above our fellow Christians. Just like Eve, we are reluctant to trust God entirely with our lives or our situations.

In his book, The Genesis Record, Dr. Henry M. Morris says that, "as soon as one begins to deny God's Word, or to question

His sovereign goodness, he is really setting himself up as his own god. He is deciding for himself the standards of truth and righteousness."

Dr. Henry M. Morris, The Genesis Record, Baker Book House, pg. 112

We practice martial arts, holistic health care, hypnotism, acupuncture, Tai chi, yoga, meditation, aromatherapy . . .we call the psychic hot lines, the angel hot lines; get our fortunes told, and opt for sensationalism as opposed to good old-fashioned communion with God as a sinner on our knees.

The greatest lie of the new age is that there is no devil, and sadly enough there are Christians who believe it. I had a preacher tell me one day, "oh I guess you can call it the devil, or you can call it bad people, or you can call it *whatever you like* . . . " Satan's biggest coupe is that he has convinced millions of Christians that he doesn't really exist, he's simply a theory, a metaphor for the bad things in this world. (Or worse yet, if he does exist, he's harmless). Wake up people! Satan himself assailed Jesus in the wilderness, (Matt. 4:1-11, Luke 4:1-13) and Jesus said, He" beheld Satan as lightening cast from heaven" (Luke 10:18). He's real, and he's here!

*   *   *   *

We still try to clothe ourselves in our own righteousness instead of God's righteousness. Just like Eve, we still succumb to the same temptations; "the lust of the eyes, the lust of the flesh, and the pride of life" (1 John 2:16).

I think it's pretty sad after all these years, Satan doesn't have to trouble himself to come up with any new ideas because we're still falling for the same *old* ones.

*   *   *   *

As far as witnessing the results of Eve's transgression; "the whole creation groaneth and travaileth in pain together..."
Rom. 8:22

Chapter 5
Examples of Ungodly Wives

Mrs. Job:
Job 2:9, 19:17, 31:10

There are only three verses in the Bible which mention Job's wife. Of the three, one is the only quotation that she is known to have rendered: "Dost thou still retain thine integrity? Curse God and die" (2:9).

Many of the writers that address Job and his wife put forth the notion that she was a good wife until hard times hit, then she simply folded under the pressure; uttered her now infamous quotation, and when the disaster subsided, remained with her husband, bore additional children, enjoyed the restoration of their material wealth, and lived happily ever after.

To give you my honest opinion, I'm not so sure . . .I have often wondered if God did not give Job a new wife; but this is only my opinion.

In the beginning, God created woman to be man's helpmeet, so this was not only Mrs. Job's position, it was also her duty.

The Bible tells us that Job was "perfect and upright, one that feared God and eschewed evil . . . "(1:1), and he practiced sacrifices *continually"* for his sons just in case they may have "cursed God in their hearts . . . " (1:5). Even God Himself described Job as "perfect and upright" there being none like him "in the earth . . . " (1:8).

We find no mention of Job's wife worshiping with him, or sacrificing with him.

Frankly, I think the character of Mrs. Job can be summed up in the one verse attributed to her: "Dost thou still retain thine integrity? Curse God and die." Could she be a more obvious tool for the devil? I don't think so; after all, it was Satan's ultimate aim to make Job so miserable that he would indeed "curse God to His face" (2:4-5).

The definition of the word *integrity* according to Funk and Wagnall is: 1. *Uprightness of character.* 2. *Unimpaired state; completeness; soundness.*

Job was the first book of the Bible that I ever read. It was during a terrible time in my marriage, where my husband and I had lost everything we had. The only things that we did not lose were our children. We lost our home, our cars, our businesses, our pets, our friends, and our self-respect because in our own eyes, we were failures. I never blamed my husband for our situation, nor did I separate myself from our situation as if it were a problem that was solely his. I certainly didn't suggest that he curse God. Furthermore, as the wife, I felt that it was my duty to encourage his hope. This doesn't mean that I was always hopeful, because I wasn't. Some days I had absolutely no hope at all, nevertheless, it was still my job to encourage *his* hope. It must be a terrible thing when a man cannot provide for his family, because every man whether he acknowledges it or not, knows that it is his obligation to provide.

Because of the swiftness and the completeness of our losses, it was obvious (even to a superficial Christian like me), that the hand of God was in this situation; that is why I picked up a Bible and began to read.

I tell you this story to make the following point: despite that hardship that Job and his wife suffered together, instead of being supportive of her husband, and considering that his grief was certainly equal to if not greater than her own, she chose to separate herself from him, and attack him in a place that only she could reach. Being his wife, she *had* to know

43

the extent of his integrity; witnessing his worship and dedication to the True and living God. She had to understand the love and reverence that Job held for Him, and she had to realize the bounty in their lives because of her husband's faithfulness.

Her utterance expresses a shallowness that many wives still mirror today; a lack of faith in the face of adversity. They are willing participants in the bounty their husbands provide, but when the cupboards are bare, and the pickings are slim, they turn their bitter tongues on their partner and lash him to death with their mouths and their hurtful words.

The Bible does not show us that Mrs. Job cared for her husband during his illness, but rather the Scriptures tell us his breath caused her to turn away from him (19:17). We find that Job cries, "All my inward friends abhorred me: and they whom I loved have turned against me" (19:19).

I can't imagine in my heart that God would restore to Job everything twofold, without giving him a wife who was twice the woman of his first wife.

She was everything a wife shouldn't be. Her obvious lack of integrity should put all of us to shame for the whole of womankind. She was shallow, bitter, hateful, selfish, and faithless. She did not share her husband's vision, nor his depth of commitment to God. It appears that she may have known *of* God, but it was painfully obvious that she did not *know* Him personally. It seems the only thing she knew of God was that if you cursed Him you would die immediately, for that was the superstition of the day.

Many writers attribute her remark to pity for her husband's situation, suggesting a way to ease his suffering. I imagine the same writers would plead the cause of Dr. Kevorkian as a Humanitarian one. Personally, I feel that Mrs. Job was of a mind that if her husband died, she would be free (for that was the Law), her suffering would be diminished, and quite possibly, she could begin her life again.

No matter what is not known about Mrs. Job, she will remain infamous because of her bitter and insensitive comment in the midst of her husband's suffering, and stand for all times, an example of a "foolish woman."

Jezebel:
1 Kings 16:31; 18:4-19; 19:1-2; 21:5-25; 2 Kings 9 Revelation 2:18-29

We come now to the woman in the Bible whose name after thousands of years is still synonymous with evil, wickedness, and idolatrous sin. Jezebel!

Many of the authors write regarding Jezebel, that she married a weak man, and manipulated him into doing her will, although when you read the Bible's account of Ahab and Jezebel, you find that really isn't the case.

Old folks used to have a saying when I was younger: "Water seeks its own level." Such was the case of Jezebel and Ahab. They were two soul mates in evil, wickedness, and idolatrous debauchery.

Ahab, the son of a wicked King whom the Bible says, "wrought evil in the eyes of the Lord, and did worse than all that were before him" (1 Kings 16:25), was found to be even more wicked than his father. "And Ahab the son of Omri did evil in the sight of the Lord above all that were before him" (1 Kings 16:30).

"And it came to pass, as if it had been a light thing for him to walk in the sins of Jeroboam the son of Nebat, that he took to wife Jezebel the daughter of Ethbaal king of the Zidonians, and went and served Baal, and worshiped him" (1 Kings 16:31).

Many times people will see what they consider to be a strong, overbearing, or demanding wife, and wonder how her husband ever puts up with her, when the reality is that it's usually her husband who is the driving force behind her.

We have Ahab who seems to have reached his zenith of wickedness, when he realizes that he can still do more! What does he do? He marries Jezebel; an idolatrous princess; daughter of a king, and a priest of Baal (Ethbaal). A match made in Hell.

I smile as I write this because Jezebel, by all worldly standards really was a good wife. She was supportive of her husband, she stood by his side through thick and thin, she indulged his whims, and nothing would keep her from giving him whatever he wanted if it were in her power to do so (1 Kings 21:1-16).

Nevertheless, Jezebel was not a godly wife. She was unscrupulous and had neither conscience nor compassion.

She was idolatrous, and a promoter of idolatry on a grand scale. Between the prophets of Baal, and the prophets of the "groves," there were eight hundred and fifty priests promoting idolatry in Israel's Northern Kingdom (1 Kings 18:19). Both Ahab's and Jezebel's wickedness seemed to possess and consume them.

Children are the products of their parents, and these two were no exception. Ahab's father was wicked and evil, and Ahab was even more wicked and evil than his father; Jezebel's father was a priest of Baal, and his daughter was a worshiper and promoter of the same. Both of them were of royal heritage, and as such, were accustomed to having their own way no matter what the cost.

The first commandment of the True and living God is "Thou shalt have no other gods before Me" (Ex. 20:3). Not only did Ahab and Jezebel have other gods "before Him," they indulged themselves as if they were gods as well.

The end of Ahab and his wife were similar inasmuch as, their ends were predicted by the prophet Elijah, (1 Kings 21:19, 23), and they ended up with the dogs to lick their blood and eat their flesh (1 Kings 22:37-38, 2 Kings 9:33, 35-36).

As a mother, Jezebel was the cause of misery and

death in the lives of her children.

It is true the Bible says that Jezebel "stirred her husband to wickedness" (1 Kings 21:25) possibly he was simply trying to keep up with her; probably he was so far in that he could no longer get out. That happens to people who have gone so far with Satan that it seems the only way they can go. Ahab seemed to have a surface knowledge of God, and a nominal fear of Him as long as he had the prophet of God there to remind him. However, on his own, he fell back into old habits and remained absorbed by the darkness in which he walked.

In conclusion, it seems the question to be asked, is "are you your husband's Jezebel?"

Do you stir your husband to wickedness for your sake? Do you encourage him to do wickedly for his own sake?

There are many pastors' and ministers' wives who indulge their husbands in extramarital sexcapades; some of them even participate with their husbands in these activities as well.

Do you indulge your husband in his whims and desires not matter how ungodly, no matter the cost incurred? Do you placate your husband as if he were a demi-god, and you his demi-goddess? Are you more interested in the gain that comes from your position, than in the giving that is required of you? Is your ministry a vocation; a means to a material end, or is it a calling on your life? Do you allow yourself to be over indulged by your church in supplying your every material need (and want), or do you "seek first the kingdom of God that all these things might be added unto you" (Matt. 6:33)? Are you more concerned with your outward appearance, than what is in your heart?

Jezebel arrayed herself fabulously before she was thrown to her death by eunuchs, and subsequently eaten by dogs (2 Kings 9:33, 35). Do you think the dogs realized they were eating *gourmet;* royal meat in designer wrappings?

Always remember, "Be not deceived; God is not mocked: for whatsoever a man soweth, that shall he also reap.

For he that soweth to his flesh shall of the flesh reap corruption; but he that soweth to the Spirit shall of the Spirit reap life everlasting"(Gal. 6:7-8).

*   *   *   *

Jezebel is also mentioned in the book of Revelation (2:18-29), as having her place in the Church of Thyatira.   I will not in the case of this book expound this section into a grand commentary since this is a handbook.

I will attempt to view this section of Scripture from three positions: [1] what was, [2] what is, and [3] what is to come.

[1] In the days of John, the city of Thyatira sat in a valley between Pergamos and Sardis. Thyatira itself was a trade city on a main thoroughfare whose economy was based on trade.

In the Book of Revelation, a woman called Jezebel is said to have called herself a "prophetess," and she taught the people to "eat things sacrificed unto idols, and to commit fornication" (verse 20).

The book of Revelation is the only book in the New Testament that is significantly "Hebrew" in its character. Its use of Hebrew figures of speech, phrases and idioms, not to mention that it bears from one end of it to the other, the character of a Hebrew prophecy shows that it is obviously addressed to a Hebrew audience. As a matter of fact, if counted, the Book of Revelation quotes or alludes to 285 Old Testament Scriptures (three times more than Matthew, which was written to the Jew specifically, and Hebrews, which as its name suggests, was also written to the Jews).

See: Commentary on Revelation by E. W. Bullinger; published by Kregel

48

Publications, pgs. 5,6.

The Hebrew word for "woman" is also the same word for "wife." Apparently, this Jezebel was the 'wife' of one of the members of the church.

She appointed herself as a prophetess and set about to teach the people "another way."

Basically she was teaching them they could still be in the world while being in the church.

In that day, many in the church made their living by trade, and salesman then; just like now, enjoyed "cementing" their deals with a few drinks and some good food. In the case of the Thyatirans, they ate and drank in the temples of the other gods, eating and drinking things that had been sacrificed to idols.

Another reason for the mixing of 'light' and 'darkness', was that the members of the church felt it would hurt them professionally if the set themselves too far apart from the "Heathens," so they mixed in for reasons of social acceptability.

The "Jezebel" in the church of Thyatira was teaching the doctrine of "compromise."

The people had biblically unsanctioned sexual liaisons, thereby committing "adultery," and they served other gods: i.e., themselves, their jobs, their money, their homes, their love interests . . . thereby, committing "idolatry" (verse 20).

[2] If you were to investigate the history of the Church, as well as the birth of the modern cults since the latter part of the 19th Century, and into this Century, you will find that many of these movements have been started by women.

There are women in the church now whose only desire is to become the Pastor and to teach other women to seize the reins of authority just as they have. They are dissatisfied and wish to incite others to dissatisfaction.

There are women in the church simply to get a chance

to have sex with the preacher or some lesser "holy" man, and they feel that they can still be godly and fornicate at the same time.

There are women who disrupt the message to speak in tongues, or prophesy out of order (1 Corinthians 14); they scream and shriek and fall out unconscious, successfully aiding Satan in stealing the message that God is sending to His people.

There are women who come to church to be worshiped for their singing voices, or their beautiful clothes, or the amount of money they tithe, or their generous gifts to the church (usually bearing their name or family name).

There are women (and men) in the church that are busy trying to incorporate New Age doctrines into the Gospel of Jesus Christ (and unfortunately, they are succeeding).

There are People in our churches that claim to receive 'revelations' from God that are not in the Bible because these revelations are not for the *common folk,* but for those that are increased in knowledge, or those that have secret knowledge.

Just like Ahab's Jezebel who brought idolatry to the Northern Kingdom and did her best to reap destruction in God's land, the spirit of Jezebel is in God's churches, consuming all that would embrace it; male and female; young and old. Always remember, Satan doesn't discriminate, only we do.

[3] Just as God declares of the Jezebel in Revelation: "And I gave her space to repent of her fornication; and she repented not.

Behold, I will cast her into a bed, and them that commit adultery with her in to great tribulation, except they repent of their deeds.

And I will kill her children with death; and all the churches shall know that I am He which searcheth the reins and hearts; and I will give unto every one of you according to your works"(Rev. 2:21-23).

So will His judgment fall on the modern day "Jezebels" that infiltrate our churches today, and all those that would follow her will receive the same judgment as she.

Repentance is available only to the living.

Herodias:
Matthew 14:3-12; Mark 6:14-21; Luke 3:19-20

Herodias was the wife of Herod Antipas, and the former wife of Phillip 1, brother of her father Aristobulus, which made Phillip her uncle in addition to being her husband. However, there seemed to be no future her marriage to Phillip, so when Herod Antipas came to visit Phillip, I imagine Herodias seduced him, causing him to think *he'd seduced her*. Herod then divorces his present wife, and subsequently marries her.

Immediately we get a picture of a sultry, sensuous woman; manipulative and beguiling. Often Herodias is compared to Jezebel, but personally, I feel that Jezebel possessed an "in your face" kind of evil, while Herodias was more like a beautifully deceiving, erotic, yet highly venomous plant, animal, or reptile. Something so toxic that as soon as you make contact with it, you know it was a mistake, but it's too late to be saved; the poison having you mostly dead *already*.

Herodias marries Herod Anitpas (her former brother-in-law), and together with his niece; her daughter (Salome) from her first marriage, moves to her husband's estate in Galilee.

Everything seems to be going smoothly until John the Baptist shows up. John is a holy man, both respected and feared by her husband Herod, whom the Bible says "observed" John, and "heard him gladly" (Mark 6:20).

John had no qualms with letting the Herod's know their marriage was against the law (Mark 6:18). This enraged Herodias causing her shame and grief, and causing her to

51

complain to her husband that John might be imprisoned.

Her husband bowed to her wishes so he thought, but truly, imprisonment was not enough for Herodias, she desired to have John killed (Mark 6:19); but the Bible said "she could not."

Unlike Jezebel, who probably could have told her husband what she wanted, and he would have fulfilled her desire, (or let her do it herself), Herodias did not have that kind of power over Herod. For even though Herod may not have feared God, he indeed feared the people. Public opinion mattered to him more than his wife's reputation.

Just like Satan beguiled Eve in the Garden of Eden, so Herodias plotted to beguile Herod into sanctioning the death of her hated accuser, John the Baptist.

She convinced her daughter to dance for Herod at his birthday celebration; instructing her that after her seduction was complete and she had Herod eating out of her hand so to speak, she was to ask for the head of John.

I imagine this was no ordinary dance, but one that incorporated "all that is in the world, the lust of the flesh, the lust of the eyes, and the pride of life" (1 John 2:16).

The dance was one of such erotic, intoxicating movements and intimations that Herod in the midst of his party guests, and being somewhat mellowed with fine wine, found himself the victim of a venomous bite. However, just as they say when a person is dying their life passes before their eyes, so the scenes that passed before the eyes of Herod had to be marvelous. He saw an intoxicating, nubile young woman who could be his for the taking; *(the lust of the eyes),* his flesh was aroused and desirous of her; *(the lust of the flesh),* and "having" her, his virility would certainly be known to his friends and colleagues who were seeing exactly what he was seeing when this young woman danced her availability to him; *(the pride of life).*

It was only after being caught up in the moment, and

shooting off his mouth, that he realized he was already a dead man (Mark 6:23-26).

Herodias was a deceitful and despicable woman who used her sexuality and sensuality to manipulate people and situations for her own gain. She wasn't even averse to using her own daughter if it meant getting what she wanted.

Herodias disappears from the annals of Biblical history as well as her daughter after the death of John the Baptist. However, the further history of Herodias can be found in the secular writings of certain historians, while Salome can still be seen dancing her erotic dance on the canvases of fine art throughout the world, and occasionally in the person of Rita Hayworth in Hollywood's version of this infamous story.

Unfortunately, I don't think Herodias is considered to have had much of an impact on the world like Jezebel did. You never hear of a woman being called a "Herodias." But the truth of the matter is that there are many Herodias' out there, women who work their wiles behind the scenes to destroy God's men of Truth with sexual weapons of warfare.

When I was younger, a woman was considered a Jezebel when she had her ears pierced, or wore red shoes or red nail polish. When I read and reread the story of Jezebel, the only sexual misconduct that she probably committed was in her idolatrous worship practices, for many idolaters had sexual orgies in the names of their gods. However, she practiced her idolatry with her husband.

Herodias was a whore, nothing more, nothing less. The woman that Solomon describes in Proverbs 5:3-5: "For the lips of a strange woman drop as an honeycomb, and her mouth is smoother than oil:

But her end is bitter as wormwood, sharp as a two-edged sword.

Her feet go down to death; her steps take hold on Hell." This is Herodias.

Part 2

So, what's my job *for real?*

Technical Information

A virtuous woman is a crown to her husband: but she that maketh ashamed is as rottenness in his bones.

Chapter 6
Church Protocol

Times have changed considerably since I was a child, and so has church protocol in America.

I can remember my grandmother taking me to Sears and Roebuck for my first pair of black patent leather "Mary Jane's." They were my "Sunday" shoes, and I was to only wear them on Sundays.

On Wednesday nights, my grandmother would cook dinner for the church Finance committee, which meant that she usually had been cooking all day, and had a vast array of mouth-watering fare including dessert(s)- for she always made two.

The family would gather (Grandpa, and Mom, her sister and husband, their three children, my brother and me); we would help my grandma pack the dinners for the church, someone would usually take the widower next door a dinner, and then we would sit down in the kitchen for our weekly family get together.

Grandpa always said "grace" and we would eat.

I can remember listening to the stories of the "old days," wondering what all of their lives were like when they were my age.

Inevitably, the conversation would always turn to church. My grandparents would always tell about the "one Sunday go to meeting" outfit they had, and were expected to keep clean and maintain. My mother and aunt would laugh and remind my grandparents they also had only one Sunday outfit they were expected to maintain and keep clean, and then they would look at us kids . . . We had several outfits, and probably more than one pair of shoes, and of course "we didn't know how lucky we were," or "how easy we had it."

Nevertheless, in the midst of our clothing bounty, we were learning that there were clothes especially set aside for worshiping God, and the clothes that were set aside, were our best!

*　　　*　　　*　　　*

When my husband would travel to Haiti on mission trips that would end with a revival or two at some of the local churches, he would always come home and relate to me the seriousness with which the Haitian people worshiped God.

He would tell me about people who lived in caves. Their children would play naked in the streets, and the women would wash themselves and their clothes in the nearby streams and creeks. They had no electricity or running water.

However, when it was time for church and worshiping God, the children would appear in crisp white outfits and shoes on their feet; their mother dressed in her best outfit would be holding their hands, and off to church they would go.

*　　　*　　　*　　　*

Sometime during the 1980's a particular denomination decided to lift their dress code, believing that if people could come to church any old kind of way, then more of them might come. Unfortunately, other denominations have since jumped on the bandwagon with a variety of dress options for worship.

*　　　*　　　*　　　*

You know, God had "not respect" unto Cain and his offering, because Cain did not give God what He asked for, he gave God what he wanted to (Gen. 4:5).

I'm afraid sometimes we have the attitude of Cain when we worship God. Sometimes we look okay when we get to church, and other times we look like we're going grocery shopping on Saturday, then planning to do a load of clothes and mop the floor afterwards.

As a pastor or minister's wife, you have an obligation to adhere to the biblical dress code. You *are* the first lady of the church, and everyone will be looking at you, because you are the one that sets the example.

In this chapter, we will attempt to address some of the major protocol pros and cons as they relate to being a pastor or minister's wife.

*　　　*　　　*　　　*

What to wear:

The Bible is very specific regarding the dress of godly women.

"In like manner also, that women adorn themselves in modest apparel, with shamefacedness and sobriety: not with broided hair, or gold, or pearls, or costly array:

But (which becometh women professing godliness) with good works." 1 Tim. 2:9-10

Well, I guess this rules out cocktail dresses, elaborate hair dos, excessive fur(s), tons of jewelry, etcetera, along with anything that is too short, too tight, and too revealing that women wear to church on Sundays. It also rules out jeans and casual wear; tennis shoes, shorts, tee shirts, and tattoos* (if possible, they should really be covered). It rules out the gobs and gobs of makeup that some of us have a tendency to wear. Save this kind of apparel for occasions outside of the church. And last but not least by any means, WEAR THE PROPER UNDERGARMENTS! How are our young girls ever going to learn how to dress properly, if we don't set the example? I'm not even going to bother to tell you how unattractive women are when everything they've got is squeezing out between their seams, or wrestling in their clothes.

Also remember; Spandex is not your friend. The only way you can possibly work up even an *acquaintance* with Spandex is if you invite its lesser-known cousin (the long line [one-piece] girdle) to join you.

Sometimes it is difficult for us to sever our Christian selves from our former worldly selves. I have seen young women who have married young pastors and ministers who are still trying to project that "sexpot" image they had when they caught their husbands. Unfortunately, the Bible instructs us to be "not conformed to this world, but to be transformed by the renewing of your mind" (Rom. 12:2). So if you are still trying to cling to a former image, its time to ask God to forgive you, and to remove the desire for worldliness from your heart. You (whether you like it or not; whether you're young or old), have an obligation to set an example of godliness for yourself, for your husband/pastor, for the congregation, and especially for the young people, who will be observing your every move.

*Re: Tattoos: "Ye shall not make any cuttings in your flesh for the dead, nor print any marks upon you: I am the Lord." LEVITICUS 19:28

Should I wear a hat?

The Scriptural ordinance regarding "head coverings" has all but become obsolete. Hat wearing has been relegated to those "holding fast to tradition," those imitating examples set by their Elders, and those wishing to make a fashion statement by making a conscientious effort to never wear the same hat two times in one year.

To answer the question, "should I wear a hat," is simple; the answer is "yes you should."

However, the real question is "why, why should I wear a hat?" The only legitimate answer to that question lay within the pages of our Holy Bible.

"But every woman that *prayeth or *prophesieth with her head uncovered dishonoureth her head: for that is even all one as if she were shaven.

For if the woman be not covered, let her also be shorn: but if it be a shame for a woman to be shorn or shaven, let her be covered." 1 Cor.11:5-6

"Why?"

There are specific reasons in the Bible as to why a woman's head would be uncovered or shorn; one reason was for mourning (Deut. 21:12), while another was when the woman was accused of committing a disgraceful act (Num. 5:18).

In order to pray or prophesy to any effect, one *must* be in the spirit (Eph. 6:18). Women have, and will continue to be valuable prayer warriors and intercessors, and to prophesy in the name of the Lord, especially in these last days (Joel 2:28, Acts 21:9).

Since "we are not ignorant of his (Satan's) devices" (2 Cor. 2:11), we should realize that Satan's goal is to make us Christians of non-effect, and we will always be of non-effect if we don't understand why we do what we do, or why it is necessary to do it God's way.

"For a man indeed ought not to cover *his* head, forasmuch as he is the image and glory of God: but the woman is the glory of the man.

For the man is not of the woman; but the woman of the man.

Neither was the man created for the woman; but the woman for the man." 1Cor. 11:7-9

All of mankind has been made after the likeness of God, inasmuch as we are created a tri-part being, having spirit, soul, and body (Heb. 4:2). However, man (the male of the species) was also created in the "image" of God (Gen. 1:26-27, 9:6), while the woman was created from the "flesh and bone" of the man to be his help meet (Gen. 2:18,22,23), and his glory (1 Cor. 11:7).

Here we come now to the verse in question:

"For this cause ought the woman to have power on *her* head because of the angels". 1 Cor. 11:10

For *what* cause ought the woman to have power on her head, *what is this power*, and what have the angels to do with it?

The "cause" or reason, is stated for the reader two times; woman was "for the man", and again, "neither was the man created for the woman, but the woman for the man."

Among other things, the number two speaks of testimony. We are told twice that the woman was created for the man. This is significant; Jesus expressed many a truth preceded by the words "verily, verily."

The Bible speaks of the testimonial value of two. We read, "In the mouth of two or three witnesses shall every word be established" (2 Cor. 13:1), we see Jesus sending His disciples out by twos (Luke 10:1), and finally, in Ecclesiastes 4:9 we read, "For two are better than one, because they have a good reward for their labor."

There is a spirit world that we can only see when the good Lord allows us a glimpse from time to time to serve His purposes. Nevertheless, the spirit world is alive and well, and operating continually, whether we can actually see the events that transpire or not.

There are things we are instructed to do in Scripture that are tangible acts, imputed for spiritual actions.

For example: Passover (Ex. 12:21-23); *real* blood from *real* lambs was smeared on *real* lintels and door posts; all tangible and visible to the eye, however, the purpose was spiritual, for it was to show the Angel of Death where *not* to go!

Therefore, the head covering is something that can be seen by the natural eye, even though it really sends a spiritual message.

Well, what spiritual message are we sending:

1. That we are obedient, and have submitted ourselves to the Word of God.

2. That we are under the power of our husband, who is under the power of Christ, who is under the power of God (1 Cor. 11:3).

3. That we are one flesh with him whom the Lord created for us.

4. That collectively, we comprise the church; the Bride of Christ, and are seen as such by both the Hosts of Heaven, and the fallen angels when we come together in fellowship. Just as above it states that we are showing our obedience to the Word of God as an individual, when we come together as a corporate body of believers, we show that we (the congregation) are being obedient to the Word of God.

In 1 Samuel 15:22, we find the words, "To be obedient is better than sacrifice." Can you imagine the power of God that must be visible to the spirit world when a congregation of *obedient* believers come together to worship Him? Can you imagine the power available to obedient believers; power to do "all things through Christ which strengtheneth me" (Phil. 4:13).

5. The un-married women show their obedience and submission to Christ whose they are, until such time as the Lord prepares for and sends to them a godly husband, whose job it will be to be her covering.

6. Lastly, if we go back to the book of Genesis, in Chapter 6, verse 2, we find fallen angels looking on the daughters of men, finding them fair, and going in unto them. We find these women conceive and bare a race of demonized humans that are an abomination to God and must be destroyed (Gen. 6:4, Num. 13:33, Deut. 2:20-21, 3:13, Josh.

12:4, 13:12, 15:8).

Furthermore, the angels that kept not their first estate were bound in chains and reserved in darkness for future judgment (Jude 6). These were not allowed to be free like their fellow fallen angels until such time as they will be sent to the lake, which burneth with fire and brimstone (Matt. 25:41), leaving us to believe that their crime was the epitome of abominations in the eyes of the Lord.

It may be that this "head covering" provides us with protection in the spirit realm that we know nothing about, for by it, we are identified as belonging to God.

"Nevertheless neither is the man without the woman, neither the woman without the man, in the Lord."
1Cor.11:11

"Why?" Because the man and the woman are one flesh, and Christians are one flesh with each other and with Christ.

"For as the woman is of the man, even so is the man also by the woman; but all things of God." 1 Cor. 11:12

Again, we receive this message two times. How important it must be for us to grasp this whole "one flesh" concept. Certainly in this day and age of self, individuality, and alternatives, being "one" with anything is foreign to us. As a matter of fact, it is so foreign to us that the Enemy has successfully packaged God's perfect plan in wrappings of imperfection, and is presently marketing it in a variety of New Age/One World Order concepts like ecumenical organizations, globalization, of monies, information, armies, nations, education, etc., the list is endless. There has been a resurgence of Paganism, and Eastern religions, and witchcraft, all of which emphasize a "oneness" with nature and/or the cosmos. We are striving to be one with everything except the one thing God created us to be one with, HIM!

The man and the woman were created to be one flesh.

Furthermore, the Christian is also to be "one flesh" with the other members of the body, and they in turn are to be "one flesh" with Christ, who is "one" with God (John 10:30). This design has been established from the beginning (Gen. 2:24), and its thread runs throughout the entire New Testament (Rom. 10:12, 1 Cor. 12:13, Gal. 3:11, Eph. 2:14-18, 4:4-6, 4:15-16).

"Judge in yourselves: is it comely that a woman pray unto God uncovered?

Doth not even nature itself teach you, that if a man have long hair, it is a shame unto him?

But if a woman have long hair, it is a glory to her: for her hair is given her for a covering." 1 Cor. 11:13-15

According to verse 15, God initially gave woman hair not only for a covering, but also for her glory. Due to the nature of the "Fall" and the subsequent judgment rendered, in order for the woman to now appear in the presence of God, it seems that a substitute is needed, and that her own glory is no longer sufficient.

Who knows, perhaps when the woman encountered Satan under the tree of the knowledge of good and evil, he told her what exquisite hair she had, and with a toss of her exquisite hair, she gave herself over to the "lust of the eyes, the lust of the flesh, and the pride of life" (1 John 2:16).

Is that not why Jesus was sent, "for all our righteousnesses are as filthy rags" before God (Is. 64:6). We could no longer come into His presence without a substitute, the ultimate substitute being Jesus Christ, the Son of God who "while we were yet sinners Christ died for us" (Rom. 5:8, 1 Pet. 3:18).

Therefore I guess the Christian response to the questioned posed by the disciple Paul in verse 13 is "no, it is not comely for a woman to pray unto God uncovered."

A pastor or minister's wife should always wear a hat, or head covering in a formal worship service, and also to visit

63

the sick when she will be praying for them in her professional capacity as a pastor or minister's wife.

I do not feel it necessary to wear a hat at informal services unless you are part of the program, and will be rendering prayer.

I know times are changing, but I truly feel it is our obligation to... "hold fast that which is good" (1 Thes. 5:22). I further believe that "*all* scripture is given by inspiration of God, and is suitable for doctrine, for reproof, for correction, for instruction in righteousness": (2 Tim. 3:16).

* Public prayer or prophesying

Where to sit:

The Bible does not address this at all. Therefore, I would suggest that you sit where *you* are most comfortable.

Many first ladies are encouraged by members of their congregation to sit in the very front of the church on the very first pew. Personally, I have found this to be one of the most un-accommodating seats in the house.

It is difficult to see the Pastor as he preaches, and it is extremely difficult to excuse yourself in case of an emergency that would require your immediate attention.

I personally try never to sit in the first pew, unless we have visiting Evangelists, or pastor's wives.

Furthermore, sitting on the first pew encourages uninvited "holy" people to sit next to you (and endeavor to talk to you through the entire service- usually about some function they want you to chair; some decision they have made, or an event they are planning; or worse yet, to *gossip*).

If you have children, it is very difficult to sit in the front of the church, because the baby will always have to "potty," or talk, or eat a little something, or have a bottle, and the older ones will begin to fidget after a while.

The teen-agers (if they are willing to sit with you at all), will also encourage their friends to sit with you as well; need I say more?

Personally, my favorite seat in the church is usually towards the back. I chose this seat for a number of reasons; first of all, I'm too far in the back for the "holy" people, so I can usually enjoy the service uninterrupted. It is an excellent position from which to critique my husband's sermon (because he will always ask me after the service "how was it?" and he will want to know if it looked like the people were listening, or if they understood what the message was telling them). It also allows him the opportunity to know if he is speaking loud enough for everyone to hear him.

From this position, if I have to, I can get the baby to the potty and back again without disturbing my fellow worshipers.

And finally, being the compulsive perfectionist that I am, I can keep an eye on the teens, who have a proclivity for running in and out of the service, or sometimes sneaking out altogether.

When visiting other churches however, you should sit as near to the front as possible. First of all, if you are compulsive like me, it will keep you in check, and prevent you from taking over someone else's job in their church.

Secondly, congregants are very proud of their Pastor and first lady, and as terrible as it may sound, they usually use the opportunity of visiting, to show off their beloved Shepherd and Shepherdess (for that is your calling).

What to Join:

Don't join anything, but be a part of everything!

As a pastor or minister's wife, you are in a unique position to move freely in all areas of the church; take advantage of it. If there is a particular area in which you have a specific interest, then give that area additional time.

Resist the urge to become an officer in this organization or that organization, remember, if we want our rewards here on earth, we'll surely get them, but then we will not have the rewards in Heaven (Matt. 6:1-4).

At times our flesh provokes us, and we seem to need notoriety; position, and importance; worse yet, we want it to be obvious to everyone else that we are important, notable, and elevated. Resist the urge!

Also, by becoming a full-fledged member and/or officer, you run the risk of becoming clique-ish. The pastor's wife needs to be available to everyone, and everyone needs to feel that she is available. People are very insecure by nature, and if they feel that you are more attentive to the members of your special group, organization, or clique, it may prevent them from coming to you in their hour of need, and your first duty to the congregation is that of a 'ministering spirit.'

"Should I, or should I not 'hang out'?"

By all means, yes. However, don't linger.

It's always nice to see the Pastor and/or his wife around the church, observing the routines and activities.

It gives people a sense of security to know that the church means more to the Pastor and his wife than simply an income.

It also lets people realize the Pastor and his wife have an interest in *everything* that is happening, no matter how small.

Just a note though, avoid the cliques and the gossip groups, just say "hi," and keep going.

Make sure you always take time to hang out with the children for a little while. You need to realize that you have the opportunity to mold a mind in godliness, so seize the moment.

Be gracious and kind:

"She openeth her mouth with wisdom; and in her tongue is the law of kindness" (Prov. 31:26).

If you are not so by nature, then I suggest that you start practicing.

Speak to people. Have a kind word to say no matter what you're going through or how bad your day has been.

Graciousness and kindness should be so much a part of you that when you fail to be either one, you immediately feel remorse (even if the person deserves neither your graciousness or kindness). Your character should be such that you are disappointed with yourself, because you know that you are not reflecting Jesus in you mannerisms.

Who should I be?

Be yourself. Am I contradicting the statement above; not at all.

Is it not our goal as Christians to be like Jesus? As you grow in grace, you will continually be changing. Each day you should be able to see more and more of Jesus in you.

Therefore, let God have His way with you that you may become that "new creature in Christ" (2 Cor. 5:17).

Chapter 7
How to handle lies, rumors, and other ugly things that may come your way

Lies and Rumors:

People are always going to talk about you and sometimes, even lie about you, and there isn't much you can do about it.

Back in the day (before you were saved), you most likely dealt with lies (and rumors, and other ugly things for that matter) all in the same way . . .

1. Confront the perpetrator with a verbal or physical attack.

2. Attack the character of the perpetrator to others; and/or

3. possibly ask the perpetrator "why?" before proceeding with measures one and two.

Unfortunately, 'being saved' leaves only one of the above-mentioned options open to you, the Christian.

Furthermore, the Bible says that not only will people lie about you, it says that you will suffer as a Christian (which includes, but is not limited to the pain that we suffer when we are talked about and lied about).

The Bible says quite a lot about how we should deal with being wronged; (Matt. 5:10-12, 39-44, Luke 17:3-4, Rom. 12:14, 20, 1 Pet. 3:16-17).

More practically speaking, you need to develop a sure fire Christian method to deal with people lying on or about you.

1. Tell God. Tell Him about it until you have been restrained enough by the Holy Spirit not to do whatever it is that you were thinking about doing first.

2. You must decide whether or not to confront the liar. Generally, I choose to ignore the liar. I don't want them to know what they said about me warrants even a minuscule portion of my attention.

By confronting them with their lie, what is to stop them from lying to you about telling the lie since you have established them as a liar from the beginning.

Besides, God has a way of rewarding both your patience and your virtue.

One day while I was sitting in Church, a young lady that my husband and I helped very much, came and sat down next to me. This particular person had said some pretty bizarre things about me, but I never confronted her with them.

As we were sitting together watching another member of the congregation sing, she leaned over and said to me, "I can't believe ___, he's got a lot of nerve still coming here after the way he talked about you guys!"

Well, I just chuckled; what could I say? She could find the splinter in his eye, but she was quite unaware of the plank in her own (Matt. 7:3).

Rumors are somewhat different than lies. A lie is something that is totally untrue, whereas, a rumor is speculation on something that you may have seen; something implied; something that *appears* to be a certain way.

The most accurate advice that could ever be given to a person regarding rumors and how to prevent them, is found in 1 Thessalonians, chapter 5, verse 22: "Abstain from all appearance of evil."

Make it difficult for rumors to begin in the first place.

Gossip:

Gossip is one of the ugly things that we encounter. Sometimes I believe that gossip is the glue that holds the church's congregation together.

People come to church on Sunday to hear the 'latest news', see the latest fashions, see the hottest couples (especially the undercover couples that no one is supposed to know about), and to be a part of the 'action.' Hearing it on the phone is only second best to being there in person.

Gossip by the way, could be considered addictive if you let yourself get carried away with it.

You may even find yourself encountering withdrawal symptoms when trying to stop. However, in order to be an effective Christian, you cannot be a gossiper!

Pray. Repent and ask God's forgiveness and deliverance from your problem- then when you find yourself getting ready to be the giver or the getter of gossip, "just say no!"

The Bible calls for us to be "grave, not slanderers, sober, faithful in all things" (1 Tim. 3:11); not "busybodies" (1 Tim. 5:13).

"The words of a talebearer are as wounds, and they go down into the inner parts of the belly" (Prov.18:8).

Infidelity:

Infidelity can also be a problem. Sometimes it's the wife, and sometimes it's the husband.

Solomon says "drink water from your own cistern" (Prov. 5:15).

If you are *that* unhappily married, then chances are you should never have gotten married in the first place.

In most cases, people who commit adultery aren't unhappy enough to get divorced, they are simply looking for love (and thrills, and attention) in all the wrong places! At least that's what they tell themselves, and some will actually believe that. Others will recognize the demon of lust for what it is.

In the event that you suspect or know that your partner is cheating on you: pray about it. God certainly has it within His power to end the unsanctioned relationship. However, you need to take into consideration that quite possibly the fault may lie with you. As a man's wife, it is your job to make sure that your husband is being taken care of in every way.

If you don't have the patience to wait on the Lord to resolve the infidelity problem, and you feel compelled to do something, please refrain from kicking the offender's butt in church. Kick it somewhere privately if you must but remember, it takes two to commit adultery, and be aware, sooner or later God will have you apologizing for your actions. The more people who see it, the more people you will have to apologize to.

As a pastor or minister's wife, you have an obligation to foster Christian unity in the church. You should never disgrace the body of believers by airing your dirty laundry in God's house, nor should you create divisiveness.

Furthermore, the Bible says "in the mouth of two or three witnesses"... (Matt. 18:16, 2 Cor. 13:1). You, your husband and the other woman make three- meet privately and work it out if possible.

Don't pretend that you don't know what's going on . . . For example, I know of a pastor that has had a wife and the same girlfriend for more than twenty years. The wife sits on her particular pew on Sundays, and the girlfriend sits on hers. This is not the answer.

When you accept this situation, and show other members of the congregation that this continuing sin is acceptable, you defeat the entire purpose of the Lord's saving grace. Jesus forgave the woman who was caught in the very act of adultery, and He told her to "go and *sin no more*" (John 5:32). (emphasis mine) He certainly didn't forgive her and then tell her to continue in her sin while He continued to forgive her of the same.

By condoning continual sin, you are making a mockery of God and His holiness; holiness that He not only stands for, but requires of us as well. "Be ye holy, for I am holy" (1 Pet. 1:16).

When you continue in sin, you are showing the congregation that you can worship and serve God; serve Satan, and still go to Heaven all at the same time. "There will be many in that day that will say Lord, Lord" . . . (Matt. 7:21-23).

Don't lie to protect the adulterer, everyone knows that you're lying, and lying is a sin. Adultery is the only legitimate reason the Bible gives us for divorce (Matt. 5:32), but this should really be your last resort, and that's only if God tells you to leave. Just a note here: God *never* tells you to leave one person for another. As a matter of fact, His word tells us " let not the wife depart from her husband: but and if she depart, let her remain unmarried, or be reconciled to her husband: and let not the husband put away his wife" (1 Cor. 7:10-11). The Bible also tells us that if we are without a spouse, we can remain unmarried and "care for the things of the Lord", when we are married (or trying to get married) we care for "the things of the world" (1 Cor. 7:34, 39-40).

If your spouse is repentant and considers that he either A- fell, or B- has a serious lust problem, then it's possible to have him anoint himself with oil; reject the demon of lust that plagues him, renounce whatever he's done to get this demon (ie. pornography, drugs, alcohol, lustful thoughts, lustful company, etc.); ask God's forgiveness, and ask God to seal those demonic doorways shut with His Holy Spirit. This will rid him of the demons and help him to stand his ground on the battlefield the next time Satan attacks him in this area again, and he will.

Infidelity and lust differ somewhat. Infidelity is when a person may have one extramarital affair, and this is usually because they feel neglected and/or taken for granted by their loved one.

There is also that group of men who feel they need more than one woman on a continuing basis, (a mistress), I believe these men are demonized by spirits that stir up the "lust of the eyes, the lust of the flesh," and above all else, "the pride of life" (1 John 2:16).

Pastors more so than ministers, are always surrounded by women who are drawn to the smell of power, it is their desire to be near the Pastor, and to serve in whatever capacity he may need them to, and I use the term *serve* loosely.

Unfortunately, these women stir up "the lust of the eyes" slithering around the Pastor and the pulpit in their slinky clothes, their low cut, see through tops, and their too tight, too short, skirts. Not to mention, they get the "Holy Ghost" just in time to fall out on the pastor's shoe tops, with their clothes in all manner of disarray. They couldn't be more obvious if they had a neon sign on their foreheads that said "I'm available for *anything*, just give me the eye."

In addition, these same women fawn and feel all over the pastor whenever the opportunity permits-rubbing and patting; picking a little string or piece of lint off his clothing; smoothing a stray hair back into place; making some type of physical contact with him. The Bible says "lay hands suddenly on no man..." (1 Tim. 5:22), and by all means, you should not allow anyone to just come along and lay their hands on you. Much can be transferred by touch.

After a woman rubs against you long enough, she begins to appeal to your flesh, ergo, the lust of the flesh is stirred.

And finally, the pride of life; it makes a man feel good

to be appreciated; especially by attractive women; and all women can be attractive if you look at them long enough, and they work at it hard enough. It strokes his ego, and women certainly know how to do that! James says "the tongue is a fire, a world of iniquity . . . it defileth the whole body, and setteth on fire the course of nature; it is set on fire of Hell" (3:6); "it is an unruley evil, full of deadly poison" (3:7).

There is always a woman out there who will tell him how great he is, and how unappreciated he is. His sermons will always be a revelation, his prayers will always be fervent and powerful, and when he sings, he will always sound like Sam Cook, or Barry White; Billy Ekstein, or Englebert Humperdink . . .

This man needs to rebuke the demons of pride and ego, and realize that he is simply God's tool (instead of being Satan's fool).

If God meant for man to have more than one woman at a time, He would have made it so from the beginning. He did not. He made one woman for the man, and He called them husband and wife, not husband and *wives.*

Lust on the other hand is really severe demonization. A person can only have a lust problem if they have lust demons. There are many ways to acquire these demons; they may have been passed down through three or four generations (Deut. 5:9-10); the person demonized may have been molested or raped as a child by either family or non-family members. This person may have been involved in watching and/or reading pornography, or participating in pornographic acts. Also, people don't realize that fornication opens doorways to demons of lust.

The point that I would like to make here is that lust has nothing to do with other women. Recently I spoke with a woman who believes her husband to be possessed by a lust demon. She expressed to me her feelings of inadequacy with regards to fulfilling her husband's desires in a woman. It was difficult to make her understand that lust has nothing to do with another woman.

Lust doesn't care if she is a blonde or brunette; young or old, fat or thin; in severe cases, lust doesn't even care if it's male or female. Lust is like a gaping mouth, which is always hungry; it eats and eats to satisfy its desire, yet it is never full. The more it eats, the more it needs, except, the needs become greater, and more varied.

Three important things are needed to be said here; first of all, the renouncing of demons must be done out loud. Jesus rejected Satan out loud (Matt. 4:10-11, Matt.16:23, Matt. 17:18, Mk. 1:25, 34, 39, Luke 9:42), and we must do the same. You do not have to be a witness to this rejection. Some of us have committed sins so gross that we can barely acknowledge them to ourselves let alone our spouses.

Although, it is better if you can anoint your husband and pray for him while he is praying for himself. Make sure you have a bottle of oil; use it all if you have to, and cover him from head to toe.

Make sure you have prayed over the oil, and have asked God to change it from its carnal use, to its spiritual use, which is the blood of Jesus. Pray through until God lets you know that its time to stop.

It is very important to have your ear finely tuned to God's voice. Read your Bible and pray up for some days before attempting this deliverance. It is important to know what you're dealing with, and only God can tell you that.

You should also anoint yourself before hand. Ask God to cleanse you with the precious blood of Jesus, and to protect you against Satan and his demons.

Secondly, I cannot stress the importance of remembering (Luke 11:24-26), one comes out and seven return. Receiving the same old demon back again will bring seven demons even stronger with him, and your last state will be worse than your first. The 'empty house' must be filled with

Jesus, or all of you anointing will be in vain.

And thirdly, you must be willing to forgive (Matt. 6:14-15)! This is probably the hardest task of all, but if you are unable to forgive him, your relationship will be doomed because nothing will change. Sooner or later he will go back to his old ways because he is getting no satisfaction from you.

In all this, you must maintain a prayer vigil, and keep a watchful eye. People who have been the victims of demons need considerable care. They must continually be prayed up. They must be taught how to maintain an open prayer line with God, and they must be taught within the confines of Scripture, how to fight back; plead the blood of Jesus; rebuking the demons, and trusting God to keep them and protect them.

If they acquired their demons through pornography, all of that material needs to be gotten rid of, even something as simple as a "girlie calendar" in their office, or at their job.

Also, you cannot be one of those people that forgives with the attitude "I'll forgive, but *I'll never forget."* That is not biblical forgiveness. When God forgives us, the Bible says that " as far as the east is from the west, so far hath He removed our transgressions from us" (Ps. 103:[10-11] 12).

We should be "wise as serpents and harmless as doves"(Matt. 10:16). The only way we can be wise is to read God's word, and the only way we can be harmless is to rest in the knowledge that our God is "able." We cannot do either if we do not have a personal relationship with Jesus.

Prejudice:

In this section, I will only address prejudice in the 'Body', the unseemliness of it, and God's reaction to it.

I was very disappointed when I first joined my husband in the ministry by the prejudice that was very obvious in the Church.

And, prejudice is not limited to one particular group. It

can be found in the Black churches, the White churches, the Latino and Asian churches; it can be found in the Baptists, the Methodists, the Episcopalians, the Southern Baptists, and the Presbyterians that comprise the body of Christ.

It is truly sad to visit a church and be made uncomfortable, or completely overlooked, simply because of the color of your skin, or the clothes you may be wearing, or the language that you speak.

I visited a church once on the Mexican Border that sat the Mexicans from Mexico in the basement, and the American Mexicans in the sanctuary.

There is always something you can find to be prejudice about in the World. However, the Bible says that we must cast this worldliness off when we join the Body of Christ (Jas. 1:27, Titus 2:12).

There is nothing more distasteful to me than to go to Church to hear a word from the Lord, only to hear the preacher preach about how 'The Man' has suppressed, oppressed, depressed, and repressed "us." Frankly, it makes it sound like the God we worship is unable to do anything for us at all.

It is equally distasteful to go to church to hear a word from the Lord, only to hear the preacher stand in the pulpit and preach about "these people" who want to join our clubs, go to our schools, join our church, and fellowship with "us."

And lastly, and certainly abhorrent are those who would twist the Scriptures to sustain their claim of Biblically imposed prejudice.

When my husband was installed as Pastor of our church, there was an audience of approximately three hundred and fifty people. There were also various pastors and bishops participating in the service.

Because of the type of ministry that we had, there was a healthy mix of drug addicts, prostitutes, and ex-cons in the congregation, as well as local officials, Black people, White

77

people, and bona-fide church people.

Well, the first Bishop stood to address the crowd and called us "you people", my husband and I looked at each other and kind of shrugged our shoulders figuring it was just one of those little social faux pas; then the second Bishop stood up and addressed us as "you people," at this point we had to cover our mouths to keep from laughing out loud.

The reaction from the other members of the congregation was rather humorous as well, for it was in question as to who the "you people" were.

The Presbyterians came up to me after the service and said how much they enjoyed it, but they had never been called "you people" so many times before.

The Methodists, Pentacostals, Baptists, Episcopalians, drug addicts, prostitutes, and ex-cons expressed the same sentiment.

Even though this can be considered a humorous anecdote, we really need to be careful of how we say things. Once the words leave our lips, we can never take them back again.

I also think it is important to realize that once we are received into the Body of Christ, that we are of a heavenly nationality. We are no longer Black or White; "Jew or Greek" (Rom. 10:12, 1 Cor. 12:13-27).

Prejudice is not acceptable to God, and you are only fooling yourself if you think you can be a Christian, and a racist, or a Christian and a bigot.

"And Miriam and Aaron spake against Moses because of the Ethiopian woman whom he had married: for he had married an Ethiopian woman.

And the Lord came down in the pillar of the cloud, and stood in the door of the tabernacle, and called Aaron and Miriam: and they both came forth.

And the anger of the Lord was kindled against them; and he departed.

And the cloud departed from off the tabernacle; and, behold, Miriam became leprous, white as snow: and Aaron looked upon Miriam, and behold she was leprous."
Num. 12:1, 5, 9, 10

*   *   *   *

Just as Phillip was translated by God to explain the Scriptures to the Ethiopian eunuch (Acts 8:27), God moves His laborers from one place to another to serve His purpose. These people join our churches hoping to continue in the service of their beloved Lord and Savior, only to find themselves met with suspicion, envy, and resentment.

Maybe a pastor, deacon, or evangelist has joined your church, ready to be obedient to their new pastor, only to find the present ministers, deacons, or evangelists less than receptive.

It could be that the new member was a Sunday school teacher or missionary. Instead of being allowed to share their talents with the congregation for the glory of the Lord, they are made to feel more like an intruder than a brother or sister in Christ.

What is the purpose for the "call to discipleship" if you really don't want any new disciples in your church?

God is not calling people to warm the pews. He is calling laborers (Matt. 9:37-38).

Rejection of the Gospel:

Many times we feel called to share the Gospel with people *we feel* need to hear it. First of all, make sure you are within the confines of God's will. There are moments in our zeal, when we want to share with everyone whether God has said so or not. We are too impatient to wait for God, so we proceed without Him figuring that He'll just catch up.

The Bible instructs us to wait on the Lord (Ps. 27:14). There are many times that I may feel someone needs some evangelizing, but I have learned to wait on the Lord. In so doing, I find that when God sends someone my way to be evangelized, or comforted, or prayed for, or instructed, if they are going to 'receive' then God has already softened their hearts.

Sometimes their heart is changed, and sometimes it isn't. *Sometimes* people are not receptive. They are apathetic, they are bored, they are rebellious, reluctant, retardant, and even hostile in response to the Gospel of Jesus Christ.

It is my personal opinion that we are living in the last days, and I believe that God is giving everyone an opportunity to be saved. It's too bad that many of them won't receive it.

Nevertheless, we are to "preach the Gospel to every creature" (Mk. 16:15). We are to "plant the seed" (1 Cor. 3:7).

Peradventure their heart be "hardened" (Ex. 7:3), God has left us with instruction: "shake off the dust of your feet" . . . (Matt.10:7-15, Mk. 6:11, Luke 9:5).

Arrogance, self-aggrandizement, hypocrisy:

The last "ugly" thing I will address is finding yourself supporting an arrogant, puffed up, lying, phony pastor or minister/husband (Matt. 6:1-8, 16-18, Matt.15:8-9, Matt.23:5-7, 11-15, 27-28).

How did you ever end up here in the first place? The wife is the "help meet." She should be equally yoked with her husband in the Word. It is your job to be your husband's friend and partner. Would you let him go out with food in his teeth, a hole in his pants, dandruff all over his shirt? No! Then why would you let him go out with his butt on his head where his brain should be.

Arrogance is quite unseemly in a pastor or minister. Besides, "which of you by taking thought can add one cubit to his stature" (Matt. 6:27)?

If your husband is a liar, discuss it with him in private

(Rev. 21:8).

If your husband is a hypocrite, I suggest you pray hard; discuss it with him in private, and let him know that as a Christian, you cannot be a partaker in his transgressions against God.

The Bible says to be subject to your husband, as he is subject to Christ. In order to be subject to Christ, Christ must be the Lord of his life. You cannot worship your own self, and satisfy your own desires, and be subject to Christ.

Christ says that we are to deny ourselves and follow Him (Matt. 16:24).

Chapter 8
Getting used to living in a fishbowl

This is something that you will definitely need to learn if you are going to survive as a pastor or minister's wife. (Haven't you noticed that people expect *you* and your family to be 'holier' than them)!

I do not have any 'pat' answers to give you regarding this dilemma that you definitely will have to face, other than verses of Scripture that will cause you to "come to yourself" (Luke 15:17a) in the event you find yourself faltering.

In public:

You will be scrutinized, so it is necessary to carry yourself accordingly, especially in the World. In church it is easy to be a Christian, because you are surrounded (more or less) by fellow Christians. However, when you come into the World, the workplace, the supermarket, your child's school, you need to realize that you must take extra precautions to present yourself as godly. Why? Because it will be in one of those places when you have forgotten who you are, or laid down your cross as some people say, that someone will see you at your worst.

In private:

You must sanctify your home! You cannot put on a godly front, and then live in an ungodly atmosphere. Your home must be relieved of anything that could or would prevent the Holy Spirit continual access to your home and heart. Remove things like Buddha cups that you may have brought home as souvenirs from Japanese restaurants; old magazines and movies that you may have just put away instead of thrown away when you became saved.

Remove alcoholic beverages in abundance; like a well stocked bar, and any kind of bar memorabilia.

Any kind of occult paraphernalia like wishing incense, amulets, crystals, dragons, wizards, gargoyles, and ethnic art (which includes local gods of other cultures), or other artifacts used in ceremonies like Shaman rattles, and beads; head gear and clothing, voodoo drums and dolls; religious icons, innocent things like Lei's from Hawaii (they are dedicated to the gods of the islands), or the ever-popular Kitchen witch.

Keep ungodly things off your television, like witch and voodoo shows where they chant in an unknown tongue, Jerry Springer and similar shows that stir up strife and confusion in your home, cartoons that promote extreme violence, or serious new age/occult messages and shows with extreme sexual content.

What does any of this have to do with living in a fishbowl? Well, if your house is in order, then you will be encouraged to live godly, whether someone sees you or not. Also, even though you think that you may have hidden your skeletons in a closet somewhere, the law of averages works against you, and sooner or later, a bone or two will fall out (Num. 32:23).

Practically speaking, by accepting God's call on your life, you can certainly expect to be observed (by friends and enemies alike, and should you chose to take my advice, you are in much more danger being observed by your friends, than you will ever be by your enemies).

*   *   *   *

"For his (God's) eyes are upon the ways of man,

and he seeth all his goings." Job 34:21

"The eyes of the Lord are in every place, beholding the evil and the good." Prov. 15:3

"Every way of a man is right in his own eyes: but the Lord pondereth the hearts." Prov. 21:2

"The heart is deceitful above all things, and desperately wicked: who can know it?
I the Lord search the heart, I try the reins, even to give every man according to his ways, and according to the fruits of his doing." Jer. 17:9-10

"But I say unto you, that every idle word that men shall speak, they shall give account thereof in the day of judgement.
For by thy words thou shalt be justified, and by thy words thou shalt be condemned." Matt. 12:36-37

"So then every one of us shall give account of himself to God." Rom. 14:2

"For we must appear before the judgement seat of Christ: that every one may receive the things done in his body, according to that he hath done, whether it be good or bad." 2 Cor. 4:10

"For he that doeth wrong shall receive for the wrong which he hath done: and there is no respect of persons." Col. 3:25

"For the word of God is quick, and powerful, and sharper than any two-edged sword, piercing even to the dividing asunder of soul and spirit, and of the joints and

84

marrow, and is a discerner of the thoughts and intents of the heart.

Neither is there any creature that is not manifest in his sight: but all things are naked and opened unto the eyes of him with whom we have to do."

Heb. 4:12-13

Psalm 139 in its entirety, (verses 1-24).

Chapter 9
Can I be a pastor's wife and still have time for God?

Yes, but you must *make* time for God. As you probably know by now, it is no easy task.

There will always be something or someone that needs your urgent, undivided attention. You will have to learn to say, "could you wait a minute?"

Here are a few tips to help you have some quality time with the Lord:

Listen to Christian radio whenever you are driving in your car. Try to avoid gospel stations and opt for stations that are broadcasting sermons or Bible studies. This way you will be thinking about God, yourself, and yourself in relation to God. You will be receiving a message.

Many Christians listen to Christian music stations, but Christian music stations will not feed you. They will make you feel good, and they will encourage you to sing along, but they will not feed you, or encourage prayer or repentance.

I find that while I drive with the Gospel on my radio station, I am encouraged to pray; to consider the message; to repent; to pray for others that I may pass along my way; and to have a Christian attitude while driving.

Recently I was riding in my car, and in the midst of prayer a young man rear-ended us. Praise God, for there was no damage done to my vehicle (and he hit us rather hard). Furthermore, I was encouraged by the Holy Spirit to simply send him on his way. I thanked God for protecting us, and I thanked him for my new, sturdy car.

You also need to cultivate some quiet time for uninterrupted communion with God. This can be anytime during the day or night that you can pray without distraction. For me it is very late at night, and into the wee hours of the morning. I am fortunate that God will wake me, and I know that I am then supposed to pray.

If you are fortunate enough to have your own private office at work, you may consider closing your door in the morning when you first arrive, and having a prayer of Thanksgiving. You may also repeat this measure at lunch-time. If you have a radio, take the opportunity to be encouraged throughout the day via Christian broadcasting.

Pray and worship with your children. This will give you time to pray, as well as encourage your children to pray.

Go to a service at someone else's church! There are many churches that have worship services and revivals during the week, take the time to visit one or two of them. This will allow you some time to worship without the responsibility of being 'the first lady'. You will be able to lay down your mantle of leadership, authority, and responsibility, and put on the mantle of a humble heart that has come to worship and commune with God.

You must learn to be creative. There is an old hymn that says, "steal away, steal away, steal away to Jesus," and that is exactly what you will have to do.

The Bible says that Satan came to steal and destroy (John 10:10), and this can be applied to your time with God. The Enemy will do his best to make sure that you will have little if any, time for God.

You may consider buying a desk calendar of Bible Scriptures, afterwards, you might place the scriptures around your office to encourage you continually, and to bring you into remembrance of who you are. Make sure you also have a Bible close at hand, and if time permits, read when you can.

Spend time with Jesus while you a cooking or doing

your housework. Think of Him, and talk to Him. Prayer doesn't always have to be formal.

About the only place that you won't have time for God is in church on Sunday mornings.

For some reason, Sundays are always our most busy and hectic days. There is so much to do before, during, and after church, I notice that God is sometimes pushed to the side.This is especially true if you are an *active* pastor or minister's wife.

There is the social time in which you are required to co-mingle with the members of the congregation. There is Sunday school at which you may be a teacher, or find yourself filling in for an absent teacher; the worship service in which you may play an active role either singing in the choir or reading Scripture or rendering prayer; finally service is over, at which time you are again required to co-mingle, and then church is over! It is then you realize that God was only in your peripheral vision, and not the object of your undivided attention.

You will not survive in the ministry without making time for God. What you do requires that you be able to HEAR God when He speaks to you. What you do becomes an impossible task, (or worse yet, a burden) if you are not filled with the Holy Spirit. It is only the Holy Spirit that allows you to be able to minister with love.

If you recall the story of the woman with the issue of blood, when she touched Jesus He felt the "virtue" go out of Him (Mk. 5:25-34). It is the same with us; if we are only 'outputting' and never 'inputting' we will find ourselves depleted, and unable to do whatever task God has set before us.

Make yourself a mental note right now to spend more time with God, no matter what it takes. Ask the Lord to make a way. You will notice the difference right away, and you will be glad!

Chapter 10
The wife as the spiritual Troubleshooter

"Thou therefore endure hardness, as a good soldier of Jesus Christ.

No man that warreth entangleth himself with the affairs of this life; that he may please him who hath chosen him to be a soldier."   2 Tim. 2:3-4

The call to be a soldier is not any different than the call to be the wife of a pastor, and the mother of his children, for you will find yourself encountering many spiritual battles.

It is the call of the wife/mother, to be the keeper of the hearth. That means it is your job to make sure that 'Sanctuary' is provided in your home. In order to accomplish this effectively, you *must* become the spiritual troubleshooter in your home.

In this chapter, I will attempt to establish exactly what "keeper of the hearth' means. I will also endeavor to address how we should prioritize what is important, and what is not.

Lastly, I will address the focus of a professional troubleshooter, and methods that should be employed to *obtain*, and *retain* 'sanctuary.'

As I write this chapter today, I have just been made aware that a good friend of mine's mother has passed away.

It has caused me to reflect on my own family, (especially my children), and what they mean to me.

As a woman, many times we are called upon to sacrifice for the benefit of others. There are moments when we look back on our lives and consider those things that we could have done, and could have been had we not sacrificed ourselves and/or our goals, for another.

The worst part of reflecting on a sacrifice, is wondering if the person or persons that you have sacrificed for, realize what you actually did for them. The answer is "probably not," at least not right away. Honestly you will be fortunate if they even realize it in your lifetime.

God prepared and sent His son to make the ultimate sacrifice for us, and many of us will never wholly realize exactly what that sacrifice entailed. There will be many who never realize the magnitude of the gift given us by the Father whose son shed His precious blood for us "that while we were yet sinners (He) Christ died for us" (Rom. 5:8).

Nevertheless, being a keeper of the hearth entails some sacrifice.

A hearth is that area in front of the fireplace where you sit to keep warm; it is where the family gathers before or after a meal, it is where the children lay to be near the warmth of the fire. Therefore, the hearth is only beneficial when there is a fire in the fireplace.

As keeper of the hearth, it is your job to keep the fire burning. It is also your job to make sure that no embers escape to fall undetected in a place where they may cause a fire. So, technically, your job is to generate security, and prevent danger.

In order to do this job effectively, it is important to be able to distinguish between things that are important, and things that are not. It is also important to be able to prioritize the important things.

In this chapter we will divide the priorities into two categories; worldly and spiritual. You will find them listed in the order of their importance.

God should be the nucleus of all of your priorities. Nothing is important if it will not award you a closer relationship with, or a better understanding of God.

Jesus says that we should seek God and His righteousness, and by doing so, God would provide our earthly (or material) needs (Matt. 6:25-34).

If you had only one opportunity to leave your daughter(s) the essentials of living wherewith she might become the keeper of hearth and home for her husband and children, what would they be?

*   *   *   *

How to live in the world, without being of the world

Know your purpose:

"...Fear God, and keep his commandments: for this is the whole duty of man(kind)."   Eccl. 12:13

Know God:

"God is not a man that he should lie; neither the son of man, that he should repent: hath he said, and shall he not do it? Or hath he spoken, and shall he not make it good?"   Num. 23:19

"For the LORD your God is God of gods, and Lord of lords, a great God, a mighty, and terrible, which regardeth   not   persons,   nor   taketh   reward";
          Deut. 10:17

"By the word of the LORD were the heavens made; and all the host of them by the breath of his mouth."
          Psalm 33:6

(Read Job, chapters 38-41)

91

"Look unto me, and be ye saved all the ends of the earth: for I am God, and there is none else.

I have sworn by myself, the word is gone out of my mouth in righteousness, and shall not return, That unto me every knee shall bow, every tongue shall swear."
Is. 45:22-23

"For my thoughts are not your thoughts, neither are your ways my ways, saith the LORD.

For as the heavens are higher than the earth, so are my ways higher that your ways, and my thoughts than your thoughts."
Is. 55:8-9

"And I say unto you my friends, Be not afraid of them that kill the body, and after that have no more that they can do.

But I will forewarn you whom ye shall fear: Fear him, which after he hath killed hath power to cast into hell; yea, I say unto you, Fear him."
Luke 12:4-5

"God is a Spirit: and they that worship him must worship *him* in spirit and in truth."
John 4:24

Fear God:

"The secret of the LORD is with them that fear him; and he will shew them his covenant."
Psalm 25:14

"The fear of the LORD is the beginning of wisdom: and the knowledge of the holy is understanding."
Prov. 9:12

Love God and keep His commandments:

"Thou shalt love the Lord thy God with all thy heart, and with all thy soul, and with all thy mind."

Matt. 22:37

"Therefore I love thy commandments above gold; yea, above fine gold.
Therefore I esteem all thy precepts concerning all things to be right; and I hate every false way."

Psalm 119:127-128

Comprehend obedience:

"Rebellion is as the sin of witchcraft, and stubbornness is as iniquity and idolatry."

1 Sam. 15:23a

"...forget not my law; but let thine heart keep my commandments;
For length of days, and long life, and peace shall they add to thee.
Let not mercy and truth forsake thee: bind them about thy neck; write them upon the tables of thine heart:
So shalt thou find favour and good understanding in the sight of God and man.
Trust in the LORD with all thine heart; and lean not unto thine own understanding.
In all thy ways acknowledge him, and he shall direct thy paths.
Be not wise in thine own eyes: fear the LORD, and depart from evil."

Prov. 3:1-7

Understand the importance of having a good character:

"A good name is rather to be chosen than great

riches, and loving favour than silver and gold."

Prov. 22:1

"Who can find a virtuous woman? For her price is far above rubies."

Prov. 31:10

"For what is a man profited, if he shall gain the whole world, and lose his own soul? Or what should a man give in exchange for his soul?"

Matt. 16:26

"And let us not be weary in well doing: for in due season we shall reap, if we faint not."

Gal. 6:9

"Abstain from all appearance of evil."

1 Thes. 5:22

Eschew evil, and realize that God is in control:

"Fret not thyself because of evildoers, neither be thou envious against the workers of iniquity.
For they shall soon be cut down like the grass, and wither as the green herb.
Cease from anger, and forsake wrath: fret not thyself in any wise to do evil."

Psalm 37:1-2,8

"When a man's ways please the LORD, he maketh even his enemies to be at peace with him."

Prov. 16:7

"If thine enemy be hungry, give him bread to eat; and if he be thirsty, give him water to drink:
For thou shalt heap coals of fire upon his head, and the LORD shall reward thee."

Prov. 25:21-22

"Be not deceived; God is not mocked: for whatsoever a man soweth, that shall he also reap.

94

For he that soweth to his flesh shall of the flesh reap corruption; but he that soweth to the Spirit shall of the Spirit reap life everlasting." Gal. 6:7-8

How to protect your family and home against the "wiles" of the devil

Know your enemy:

"Now there was a day when the sons of God came to present themselves before the LORD, and Satan came also among them.

And the LORD said unto Satan, Whence comest thou? Then Satan answered the Lord, and said, From going to and fro in the earth, and from walking up and down in it." Job 1:6-7

"How art thou fallen from heaven, O Lucifer, son of the morning! *how* art thou cut down to the ground, which didst weaken the nations!

For thou hast said in thine heart, I will ascend into heaven, I will exalt my throne above the stars of God: I will sit also upon the mount of the congregation, in the sides of the north:

I will ascend the heights of the clouds; I will be like the most High.

Yet thou shalt be brought down to hell, to the sides of the pit.

They that see thee shall narrowly look upon thee, *and* consider thee, *saying, Is* this the man that made the earth to tremble, that did shake kingdoms;

That made the world a wilderness, and destroyed the cities thereof; *that* opened not the house of his prisoners?" Is. 14:12-17

"Son of man, take up a lamentation upon the king of Tyrus, and say unto him, Thus saith the Lord God; Thou sealest up the sum, full of wisdom, and perfect in beauty.

Thou hast been in Eden the garden of God; every precious stone was thy covering, the sardius, topaz, and the diamond, the beryl, the onyx, and the jasper, the sapphire, the emerald, and the carbuncle, and gold: the workmanship of thy tabrets and of thy pipes was prepared in thee in the day that thou wast created.

Thou art the anointed cherub that covereth; and I have set thee so: thou wast upon the holy mountain of God; thou hast walked up and down in the midst of the stones of fire.

Thou wast perfect in thy ways from the day that thou wast created, till iniquity was found in thee.

By the multitude of thy merchandise they have filled the midst of thee with violence, and thou hast sinned; therefore will I cast thee as profane out of the mountain of God: and I will destroy thee, O covering cherub, from the midst of the stones of fire.

Thine heart was lifted up because of thy beauty, thou has corrupted thy wisdom by reason of thy brightness: I will cast thee to the ground, I will lay thee before kings, that they may behold thee.

Thou hast defiled thy sanctuaries by the multitude of thine iniquities, by the iniquity of thy traffick; therefore will I bring forth a fire from the midst of thee, it shall devour thee, and I will bring to ashes upon the earth in the sight of them that behold thee.

All they that know thee among the people shall be astonished at thee: thou shalt be a terror, and never shalt thou be any more."   Eze. 28:12-19

"And he shewed me Joshua the high priest standing before the angel of the LORD, and Satan standing at his right hand to resist him."   Zech. 3:1

"And he (Jesus) said unto them, I beheld Satan as lightening fall from heaven."   Luke 10:18

"Ye are of your father the devil, and the lusts of your father ye will do. He was a murderer from the beginning, and abode not in the truth, because there is no truth in him. When he speaketh a lie, he speaketh of his own: for he is a liar, and the father of it."   John 8:44

"And supper being ended, the devil having now put into the heart of Judas Iscariot, Simon's son, to betray him;"   John 13:2

"For such are false apostles, deceitful workers, transforming themselves into apostles of Christ.
And no marvel; for Satan himself is transformed into an angel of light.
Therefore it is no great thing if his ministers also be transformed as the ministers of righteousness; whose end shall be according to their works."   2 Cor. 11:13-15

"Be sober, be vigilant; because your adversary the devil, as a roaring lion, walketh about seeking, whom he may devour":   1 Pet. 5:8

"Beloved, believe not every spirit, but try the spirits whether they are of God: because many false prophets are gone out into the world.
Hereby know ye the spirit of God: Every spirit that confesseth that Jesus Christ is come in the flesh is of God:
And every spirit that confesseth not that Jesus Christ is come in the flesh is not of God: and this is that

spirit of antichrist, whereof ye have heard that it should come; and even now already is it in the world."

1 John 4:1-3

"And the devil that deceived them was cast into the lake of fire and brimstone, where the beast and the false prophet *are,* and shall be tormented day and night for ever and ever."

Rev. 20:10

Abstain from all things that are an abomination unto the Lord:

"Ye shall not eat any thing with the blood: neither shall ye use enchantment, nor observe times.

Ye shall not round the corners of your heads, neither shalt thou mar the corners of thy beard.

Ye shall not make any cuttings in your flesh for the dead, nor print any marks upon you: I am the Lord."

Lev. 19:26-28

This Scripture is addressing many things that we are guilty of today. We eat our meat rare or raw as in the case of beef tartar. We rub the blue dot in the Enquirer, get our fortunes told, carry and wear amulets and good luck charms. We read our horoscopes (observing the times), and shave and cut various symbols in our hair and beards. We cut our flesh and get tattoos.

"Regard not them that have familiar spirits, neither seek after wizards, to be defiled by them: I *am* the LORD thy God."

Lev. 19:31

"If a man lie with mankind, as he lieth with a woman, both of them have committed an abomination; they shall surely be put to death; their blood *shall be* upon them."

Lev. 20:13

"A man also or woman that hath a familiar spirit, or that is a wizard, shall surely be put to death: they shall

98

stone them with stones: their blood *shall be* upon them."

"The graven images of their gods shall ye burn with fire: thou shalt not desire the silver or gold that is on them, nor take it unto thee, lest thou be snared therein: for it is an abomination to the LORD thy God.

Neither shalt thou bring an abomination into thine house, lest thou be a cursed thing, like it, and thou shalt utterly abhor it; for it is a cursed thing." Deut. 7:25-26

We bring all kinds of things home with us like busts of our ethnic ancestors, statues of foreign gods, icons, items used in occult practices, eastern statues of gods that come with our exotic drinks, Native American dream catchers, South American worry dolls, and a plethora of other things that we have no business with. You should read the account of Achan in the seventh chapter of the book of Joshua.

"Ye are the children of the LORD your God: ye shall not cut yourselves, nor make any baldness between your eyes for the dead." Deut. 14:1

Body piercing has also become very fashionable. In reality, it is simply a form of self-mutilation. The jewelry that accompanies this fashion statement is usually silver, steel, or other silver colored metals- maybe it's just me, but I've noticed that witches, satanists, heavy metal freaks, and outlaw bikers all favor silver jewelry. As a matter of fact, books on practicing witchcraft specify silver jewelry for certain types of spells.

Our children imitate these things right down to the jewelry preference, and really don't know what they're saying about themselves, or the doorways they have opened for demonization.

"There shall not be found among you *any one* that maketh his son or his daughter to pass through the fire, or that useth divination, or an observer of the times, or an enchanter, or a witch,

Or a charmer, or a consulter with familiar spirits, or a wizard, or a necromancer.

For all that do these things *are* an abomination unto the LORD":
Deut. 18:10-12a

"Cursed be the man that maketh any graven or molten image, an abomination unto the LORD, the work of the hands of the craftsman, and putteth it in a secret place. And all the people shall answer and say, Amen."
Deut. 27:15

"Know ye not that the unrighteous shall not inherit the kingdom of God? Be not deceived: neither fornicators, nor idolaters, nor adulterers, nor effeminate, nor abusers of themselves with mankind,

Nor thieves, nor covetous, nor drunkards, nor revilers, nor extortioners, shall inherit the kingdom of God."
1 Cor. 6:9-11

"Flee fornication. Every sin that a man doeth is without the body; but he that committeth fornication sinneth against his own body."
1 Cor. 6:18

How to protect yourself:

"And thou shalt take the anointing oil, and anoint the tabernacle, and all the vessels thereof: and it shall be holy."
Ex. 40:9

"And he (Jesus) healed many that were sick of divers diseases, and cast out many devils; and suffered not the devils to speak, because they knew him."
Mark 1:34

Jesus gave us the power to rebuke the works of the devil in His name, but we do not exercise it, nor do we anoint ourselves, and our homes with oil, and ask for protection.

The Bible gives us many examples of how to exercise this power in order that we may stand against the powers of darkness. The following Scriptures not only show us the power of Jesus, but they also show us the power we have in His name.

"And Jesus rebuked the devil; and he departed out of him: and the child was cured from that very hour."

Then came the disciples to Jesus apart, and said, Why could we not cast him out?

And Jesus said unto them, Because of your unbelief: for verily I say unto you, If ye have faith as a grain of mustard seed, ye shall say unto this mountain, Remove hence to yonder place, and it shall remove; and nothing shall be impossible unto you.

Howbeit this kind goeth not out but by prayer and fasting." **Matt. 17:18-21**

"He that believeth and is baptized shall be saved; but he that believeth not shall be damned.

And these signs shall follow them that believe; In my name shall they cast out devils; they shall speak with new tongues;

They shall take up serpents; and if they drink any deadly thing, it shall not hurt them; they shall lay hands on the sick, and they shall recover."

Mark 16:16-18

"And he (Jesus) stood over her, and rebuked the fever; and it left her: and immediately she arose and ministered unto them." **Luke 4:41**

"Behold, I give unto you power to tread on serpents and scorpions, and over all power of the enemy: and nothing shall by any means hurt you."　　Luke 10:19

"And the Lord said, Simon, Simon, behold, Satan hath desired to have you that he may sift you as wheat:

But I have prayed for thee, that thy faith fail not: and when thou art converted, strengthen thy brethren."
Luke 22:31-32

"For unclean spirits, crying with loud voice, came out of many that were possessed *with them:* and many taken with palsies, that were lame, were healed."
Acts 8:7

"And it came to pass, as we went to prayer, a certain damsel possessed with a spirit of divination met us, which brought her masters much gain by soothsaying:

The same followed Paul and us, and cried, saying, These men are the servants of the most high God, which shew unto us the way of salvation.

And this did she many days, But Paul, being grieved, turned and said to the spirit, I command thee in the name of Jesus Christ to come out of her. And he came out the same hour."　　Acts 16:16-18

"Neither give place to the devil."　　Eph. 4:27

"And have no fellowship with the unfruitful works of darkness, but rather *reprove* them."
Eph. 5:11

"Put on the whole armor of God, that ye may be able to stand against the wiles of the devil.

For we wrestle not against flesh and blood, but against principalities, against powers, against the rulers of the darkness of this world, against spiritual wickedness in high *places."* Eph. 6:11-12

"Let no man beguile you of your reward in a voluntary humility and worshiping of angels, intruding into those things which he hath not seen, vainly puffed up by his fleshly mind." Col. 2:18

"Prove all things; hold fast that which is good." 1Thes. 5:21

"Take heed unto thyself, and unto the doctrine; continue in them: for in doing this thou shalt both save thyself, and them that hear thee." 1 Tim. 4:16

"Lay hands suddenly on no man, neither be partaker of other men's sins: keep thyself pure." 1 Tim. 5:22

"...avoid profane and vain babblings, and oppositions of science falsely called: 1 Tim. 6:20b

"Submit yourself therefore to God. Resist the devil and he will flee from you." Jas. 4:7

"Is any sick among you? Let him call for the elders of the church; and let them pray over him, anointing him with oil in the name of the Lord: Jas. 5:14

The wages of sin:

"For the wages of sin is death, but the gift of God is eternal life through Jesus Christ our Lord." Rom. 6:23

*   *   *   *

The focus of a professional troubleshooter is very narrow. They are called when there is an obvious problem. The problem can already be identified, but more than likely, the caller realizes there is a problem, but is unable to identify it, or its source.

The objective of the troubleshooter is to identify the problem and its source, and to resolve the problem as soon as possible.

Spiritual troubleshooting is a little different inasmuch as, the troubleshooter must rely on God, and His powers in order to insure effective and positive resolution.

The Scriptures that have been listed in this chapter, together with fervent prayer will allow you to be the effective keeper of hearth and home; as well as the spiritual trouble-shooter that one must be in these last and evil days.

Chapter 11
Some Do's and Don'ts

Do- be as much of yourself as you can be.

It is better to just keep quiet, than to pretend to be someone else. Sooner or later the real you is going to come out.

Do- learn!

Your husband deserves a partner who is equally yoked with him.

Do- cultivate your own personal relationship with Jesus.

Do- seek God's plan or ministry for your own life.

Your ministry may be to support your husband's ministry. Do the best you can, it is a very important job! Remember, Jesus sent the disciples out in twos (Luke 10:1).

Do- be a doer of the word, and not just a hearer (Jas.1:22)!

Do- have some quiet time for yourself and your family.

Do- be obedient to your husband!

By nature, human beings seem to be a rebellious lot.

When we are young, we dream of being old enough not to be subject to our parents, (and yet we get angry when our children do not wish to be subject to us).

When we get married, we take a cursory attitude when repeating the wedding vows, never considering what they truly say, and never having any intention of honoring the covenant that we are making "in the eyes of witnesses, and before God."

I have on occasion listened to Christian broadcasts that read questions from female listeners regarding the extent of obedience (or subjection) they are supposed to extend to their husbands.

God says that we are to be "subject to our husbands as he is subject to Christ" (1 Cor. 11:3).

If you think your husband is unsaved the Bible says, "Likewise, ye wives, be in subjection to your own husbands; that, if any obey not the word, they also may without the word be won by the conversation of the wives"; (1 Pet. 3:1).

When you think your husband is an idiot, take it to the Lord in prayer. When you feel your husband is making unjust demands upon you, take it to the Lord in prayer. Don't be surprised when God answers you back that the problem is not with him, but with you.

I have been married for quite a while. Sometimes my husband and I agree, and sometimes we don't. Instead of having a heated argument, we each (separate from each other), take it to the Lord in prayer; God always straightens it out.

I mention to you that I have been blessed with two godly friends. I have always considered them stronger Christians than myself because it seemed that they were always praying for me and my problems; not to mention the fact that their lives always appeared to have more order than my own. (You should never look with the natural eye for you will oftentimes be deceived).

Nevertheless, one particular day I called one of my friends to see how she was, and she began to cry. I had never heard her cry before, and I was completely devastated by her tears. She said her husband was in the hospital and although the prognosis was not very good, God had not yet put it in her spirit that he was dying.

She asked if I would send my husband to see him, and although she did not say it, she knew that my husband possessed the gifts of healing.

I asked my husband if he would go. He did, and he came back and gave me an answer that I didn't want o hear.

He told me that he spoke with this man (who was a deacon of many years), and he brought him into remembrance of who he was in Christ, "but," he also told me, "he is dying."

My flesh rebelled instantly, after all, what was I going to tell my friend if she should ask me what my husband felt when he touched him.

I begged him to go back again. He said to me, "no matter *how* many times I go back there, He is dying ..."

The spirit of rebellion said, "go to the hospital and pray for him yourself-take your oil."

The next day, I got in my car and drove to the hospital with my oil.

As soon as I stepped out onto the pavement, I knew I was wrong. I knew that I was so wrong that immediately I confessed to God my wrongdoing, and asked him that when I prayed, if He would do the talking.

Feeling horribly convicted, I rode the elevator to his floor, and got off.

When I saw him, he was in a coma, and had been for about two days. I felt terrible for my friend, and completely helpless, not to mention the fact that when I went home and told my husband what I had done, he would know that I had been disobedient.

I took out my oil; again I asked God to speak for me. I prayed, and as I prayed, I anointed his room. Afterwards, I again looked at her husband lying there. I put the oil on my finger and anointed his forehead. He opened his eyes, looked at me and smiled.

I looked at him and I said, "God sent me to tell you to get ready to go home. He is not going to leave you here like this..."

I left feeling a combination of relief (because I was leaving that depressing room), and conviction (because of my disobedience).

This was on a Friday afternoon. Bright and early Monday morning I called my friend. I was expecting her to tell me how much better her husband was doing, and that he would be home soon . . .

I said, "hey, how's your husband?" She said, Oh ___, my husband died on Saturday morning." I was speechless; how foolish I'd been.

She then proceeded to tell me that he had rallied from his previous condition to spend Saturday talking with her and saying all the last minute things that people say to each other.

I didn't dare tell her of my disobedience. I hung up the phone and I cried.

As I sat there at my desk feeling stupid, God brought to my remembrance the words I had spoken on that Friday afternoon. "God sent me to tell you to get ready to go home", and verily that is exactly where he went.

I was reminded of the time that Paul decided to go to Rome before his trip had been sanctioned by God: he was beaten by the Jews in Jerusalem, and ended up in Jail in Caesarea for two years before ever seeing Rome. Even so, his jail time was used to God's glory, for he was transferred from the jail in Caesarea to the jail in Rome, and we Saints are the beneficiaries, having received from his hand, the *Epistle to the Romans*.

I told my husband after the fact, what happened. He didn't say "I told you so" but he could have. Instead, he

108

comforted me in my foolishness and told me that he understood.

Wives be obedient! You may not always agree or understand, but do it anyway. Obedience seems to work out best not only for you and your family, but also for the good of the 'Body' in general.

Don't- give up!

Don't- be afraid to admit being tired or disgusted; dismayed, disappointed or even disillusioned; sometimes it happens. Take it to the Lord in prayer.

Don't- be afraid to confront your husband if he is doing, or considering doing something ungodly.

Don't- air your dirty laundry in Church!!!!!!

I have never been able to understand why, when people want revenge on someone in the church they feel has wronged them, they are willing to destroy the entire church just to get back at them . . . **don't** be that kind of person.

Don't- chose your close friends from within the congregation.

I hate to be the one to tell you, but it is imperative that you never chose your close friend(s) or confidants from within your congregational body. You will find your secrets betrayed, and your friends fickle. This doesn't mean that you can't share a personal moment, or a humorous anecdote. It doesn't mean that you can't go out to dinner, or that they can't visit your home, it simply means exercise caution. There is more at stake than just your personal business. What you tell someone may affect how they receive your husband as their pastor, it may affect how you are received as the first lady of the church, it may affect how someone does or does not receive the Gospel, it may affect whether they become or remain a productive member of the church, or they become the Devil's tool of disruption.

As a pastor's wife, you have to maintain a certain professionalism. Many times you will be called upon to counsel, or to instruct the women of the church in godly behavior. It is much easier to do this if you have not had an intimate relationship with them. They are more accepting of your advice, counsel, and instruction. However, this does not mean that people should feel your reluctance to be intimate with them. Everyone that encounters you should feel the love of Jesus flowing from your spirit, and that they have your undivided attention.

Don't be one of those pastors' or ministers' wives that immediately flee the scene as soon as the service is over, or one of those wives that 'turn off' when the service is over, so that when people come to talk to you they are confronted by a blast of cold air. Whether you like it or not, you have a responsibility. Jesus said that you should 'love your neighbor as yourself.' This does not mean that you have to *like* them, but it does mean that they are entitled to some semblance of Christian love.

Ask God to send you someone who will be your prayer partner, and your friend. Everyone needs someone to talk to sometimes, or someone to share their burdens with. (It's better if they are members of another church). Let God chose for you.

I am fortunate enough to have two very good, godly friends who are not members of my church. In most cases, we never talk unless there is a problem in one of our lives. Speaking for myself, when I talk to them, I am not ashamed to cry, or to appear less than perfect. I don't have to worry if they are going to judge me or placate me; if I'm right, they tell me, and if I'm wrong they tell me.

Don't- ever be a stumbling block (Lev. 19:14)!

I can remember riding in the car with my father as he was giving my husband and I a ride to a church where my husband was to be the speaker of the hour that afternoon.

We were trying to talk my father into staying for the service. I will never forget his answer to me, and I have over the years tried never to have this effect on anyone. He said, "what are these guys going to tell *me*? This one gambles, that one has a wife and a girlfriend that he's had for twenty-five years; *he's* a homosexual, so what have they got for me?" I was dumbfounded. There was no answer that I could give him.

I could have given him the *mature* Christian answer; "look neither right nor left, but keep your eyes focused on the cross," but that answer was no good for him, nor will it be good for anyone else that shares his feelings.

Whether we like it or not, people will look at us, and how we present ourselves will sometimes determine whether or not they will accept Jesus as their Lord and Savior. It is indeed a heavy burden to carry, but since we accepted our position in the church, we must also accept the fact that we are to set godly examples for the lost. We are to be that "light of the world; that city set on a hill that cannot be hidden" (Matt. 5:14).

Don't- forget that you are a steward of people's confidences! Don't be a blabbermouth!

Don't- be afraid to smell like sheep!

Many of us want to reap the benefits of being shepherds, but we don't want to smell like the sheep!

Jesus was the Great Shepherd. While he was in the flesh, He continually walked among the sheep, He was surrounded by lepers, fornicators, drunkards, adulterers,

111

hypocrites, and those that were unclean.

When He hung on the cross for our sins, He was covered with so much of our vile filth, that God in Heaven darkened the sky (Matt. 15:33, Luke 23:44) so that the bruisings He bore for our "iniquity" (Is. 53:4-6, 10-12) could not be seen by human spectators. Furthermore, God turned His face so far away from the stench of our sins that poor Jesus cried, "My God, my God, why hast thou forsaken me (Matt. 27:46, Mk. 15:34)?"

F. B. Meyer writes of this darkness in his commentary on the Gospel of John.

"For three hours it lasted, and was a befitting emblem of the darkness that enveloped his Soul when He who knew no sin was made to be sin for us..."

F. B. Meyer, Gospel of John, published by Christian Literature Crusade 1970, page 351.

Chapter 12
The Power of Prayer

Jesus said unto him, "If thou canst believe, all things are possible to him that believeth."   **Mark 9:23**

I believe this to be the crux of receiving everything that Jesus says His Father in Heaven has for us. It's funny that it can be summed up in such an unimposing and simple statement made by our Lord and Savior, nevertheless, it is the absolutely most difficult thing in the 'world' to do.

We pray and we worry. We pray and we wonder. We pray and we waiver. We pray and we doubt. We pray, but we don't believe.

"Oh God have mercy on us; help thou our unbelief; in Jesus' most holy and powerful and merciful name.

Amen"

Prayer is a must for a pastor or minister's wife. It is your lifeline, your sanity, your hope; it is the only thing that will ever be true in the world in which you have chosen to live.

Once you accept Jesus, and have set your sights on things above, you automatically become a stranger in a strange land. You walk in this world with a giant target on your back for the enemy and his minions to see; you walk in a world that is enmity with God (Jas. 4:4).

"All things whatsoever ye shall ask in prayer,

*believing, ye shall receive." Matt. 21:21

"Likewise the Spirit also helpeth our infirmities: for we know not what we should pray for as we ought: but the Spirit itself maketh intercession for us with groanings which cannot be uttered." Rom. 8:26

"Rejoicing in hope; patient in tribulation; continuing instant in prayer"; Rom. 12:12

"Be careful for nothing; but in everything by prayer and **supplication with thanksgiving let your requests be made known unto God.
And the peace of God which passeth all understanding, shall keep your hearts and minds through Christ Jesus." Phil. 4:6-7

"Pray without ceasing." 1 Thes. 5:17

"I will therefore that men pray everywhere, lifting up holy hands, without wrath and doubting." 1 Tim. 2:8

"And this is the confidence that we have in him, that, if we ask any thing according to his will, he heareth us:
And if we know that he hear us, whatsoever we ask, we know that we have the petitions that we desired of him." 1 John 5:14-15

The Bible is our example, and our instruction for successful Christian living.
Just as Jesus took time to steal away to God for prayer. We must follow His example:
"And he withdrew himself into the wilderness, and

114

prayed."   Luke 5:16

"And it came to pass in those days, that he (Jesus) went out into a mountain to pray, and continued all night in prayer to God."   Luke 6:12

While we are praying for ourselves, it is important to realize that we must also pray for others, especially those in the household of faith:

"Praying always with all prayer and supplication in the spirit, and watching thereunto with all perseverance and supplication for all saints;   Eph. 6:18

As pastors' and ministers' wives, we are also called upon to pray for others. If we cannot truly believe, can we truly expect results?

We will all experience moments of doubt, for it is the enemy's job to assail us with doubt the moment our prayers are sent Heavenward.

John the Baptist was born for the sole purpose of telling the world that Jesus Christ the Messiah was coming (Luke 1:17), yet, when he was imprisoned by Herod, and awaiting execution, his mind was assailed by the enemy, and he began to doubt. So much so, that he sent his disciples to Jesus to make sure that He truly was the Messiah (Matt. 11:2-6, Lk. 7:18-23).

Even the best of us will doubt sometimes, but we must bring every thought into submission (2 Cor. 10:5), if we are to be effective in the ministry to which we have been called.

Prayer is the key. We must remember to "pray without ceasing," if we are to be able to maintain.

Whether we want to hear it or not, according to the Scriptures, we are indeed living in the 'last days.' It would be a shame that we who share the Gospel with others would be caught sleeping and unprepared, instead of found waiting, and watching unto prayer as the Bible instructs.

"But the end of all things is at hand: be ye therefore sober, and watch unto prayer." 1 Pet. 4:7

Prayer is a powerful tool, and a powerful weapon. Following the examples set forth in the Scriptures we can be powerful tools for God on this earth.

"And Jesus rebuked the devil; and he departed out of him: and the child was cured from that very hour.
Then came the disciples to Jesus apart, and said, Why could not we cast him out?
And Jesus said unto them, Because of your unbelief: for verily I say unto you, If ye have faith as a grain of mustard seed, ye shall say unto this mountain, Remove hence to yonder place; and it shall remove; and nothing shall be impossible unto you.
Howbeit this kind goeth not out but by prayer and fasting." Matt. 17:18-21

"Is any among you afflicted? Let him pray. Jas.5:13a

"Is any sick among you? Let him call for the elders of the church: and let them pray over him, anointing him with oil in the name of the Lord:
And the prayer of faith shall save the sick, and the Lord shall raise him up; and if he have committed sins they shall be forgiven him." Jas. 5:14-15

A word of precaution:

"Ye ask, and receive not, because ye ask amiss, that ye may consume it upon your lusts." Jas. 4:3

*Believe: To accept as true on testimony or authority; to be sure of the existence or truth of anything.

** Supplication: To seek humbly by earnest prayer; to pray to grant a favor.

Chapter 13
In Case of Emergency

I consider the following subjects emergencies for the simple fact that one or more of these in your life will completely incapacitate you, and render your ministry totally useless.

Another reason I consider these things such emergencies, is because they are insidious; they sneak up on you when you're not looking; and like Cancer, if you are not fortunate enough to have the benefit of early detection; they may be spiritually terminal.

Of the Fleshly Kind:

<u>Sloth:</u> Disinclination to exertion; laziness. (Slothful: sluggish; lazy; indolent).
"He also that is slothful in his work is brother to him that is a great waster." Prov. 18:9

"Slothfulness casteth into a deep sleep; and an idle soul shall suffer hunger." Prov. 19:15

"The desire of the slothful killeth him; for his hands refuse to labor." Prov. 21:25

"Therefore let us not sleep, as do others; but let us watch and be sober." 1Thes. 5:6
"And we desire that everyone of you do shew the

same diligence to the full assurance of hope unto the end;

That ye be not slothful, but followers of them through faith and patience inherit the promises."
Heb. 6:11-12

Gluttony: The act or habit of eating to excess. (Glutton: One who gluts himself with food and drink).

"Be not among winebibbers; among riotous eaters of flesh:

For the drunkard and the glutton shall come to poverty: and drowsiness shall clothe a man with rags."
Prov. 23:20-21

"Hast thou found honey?

Eat so much as is sufficient for thee, lest thou be filled therewith, and vomit it." Prov. 26:16

Envy: To feel a grudge toward another on account of coveting what he possesses.

"Envy thou not the oppressor, and chose none of his ways." Prov.3:31

"A sound heart is the life of the flesh: but envy the rotteness of the bones." Prov.14:30

"Again, I considered all travail, and every right work, that for this a man is envied of his neighbor. This is also vanity and vexation of spirit." Eccl. 4:4

"Fret not thyself because of evildoers, neither be thou envious against the workers of iniquity." Ps. 37:1

"For wrath killeth the foolish man, and envy slayeth the silly one." Job 5:2

119

"For he (Jesus) knew that the chief priests had delivered him for *envy*." Mk. 15:10

Of the Worldly Kind:

Pride: Undue sense of one's own superiority.
"But when his heart was lifted up, and his mind hardened in pride, he was deposed from his kingly throne, and they took his glory from him": (Belshazzar) Dan. 5:20

"Talk no more so exceedingly proudly, let not arrogancy come out of your mouth: for the Lord is a God of knowledge, and by him actions are weighed." 1 Sam. 2:3

"Be of the same mind one toward another. Mind not high things, but condescend to men of low estate. Be not wise in your own conceits." Rom. 12:16

"Not a novice lest being lifted up with pride he fall into condemnation of the devil." 1 Tim. 3:6

Lust: To have passionate or inordinate desire; inordinate desire for carnal pleasure.
"So I gave them up unto their own heart's lust: and they walked in their own counsels." Ps. 81:12

"But I say unto you, that whosoever looketh on a woman to lust after her hath committed adultery with her already in his heart." Matt. 5:28

"And they that are Christ's have crucified the flesh with the affections and lusts." Gal. 5:24

120

"But they that will be rich fall into temptation and a snare, and into many foolish and hurtful lusts, which drown men in destruction and perdition."   1 Tim. 6:9

"Flee also youthful lusts: but follow righteousness, faith, charity, peace, with them that call on the Lord out of a pure heart."   2 Tim 2:22

"Teaching us that denying ungodliness and worldly lusts, we should live soberly, righteously, and godly, in this present world."   Titus 2:12

"But every man is tempted, when he is drawn away of his own lust, and enticed."   Jas. 1:14

"Dearly beloved, I beseech you as strangers and pilgrims, abstain from fleshly lusts, which war against the soul;   1 Pet. 2:11

"For all that is in the world, the lust of the flesh, the lust of the eyes, and the pride of life, is not of the Father, but is of the world.
And the world passeth away, and the lust thereof: but he that doeth the will of God abideth forever."   1 John 2:17-18

"These are murmurers, complainers, walking after their own lusts; and their mouth speaketh great swelling words, having men's persons in admiration because of advantage."   Jude 16

"How that they told you there should be mockers in the last times, who should walk after their own ungodly lusts.
These be they who separate themselves, sensual,

<u>Greed:</u> Eager and selfish desire; avarice. [Avarice: passion for riches; covetousness].

"He that is greedy of gain troubleth his own house; but he that hateth gifts shall live." Prov. 15:27

"He coveteth greedily all the day long: but the righteous giveth and spareth not." Prov. 21:26

"Yea, they are greedy dogs which can never have enough, and they are shepherds that cannot understand: they all look to their own way, everyone for his gain, from his quater." Is. 56:11

"In thee have they taken gifts to shed blood; thou hast taken usury and increase, and thou hast greedily gained of thy neighbors by extortion, and hast forgotten me, saith the Lord GOD.

Behold, therefore I have smitten mine hand at thy dishonest gain which thou hast made, and at thy blood which hath been in the midst of thee." Eze. 22:12-13

"Not given to wine, no striker, not greedy of filthy lucre; but patient, not a brawler, not covetous". 1 Tim. 3:3

"Woe unto them! For they have gone the way of Cain, and ran greedily after the error of Balaam for reward, and perished in the gainsaying of Core." Jude 11

Of the Spiritual Kind:

<u>Anger:</u> Violent, vindictive passion; sudden and strong displeasure; wrath; [Wrath: Determined and lasting anger;

122

extreme passion; rage].

"Cease from anger, and forsake wrath: fret not thyself in any wise to do evil."   Ps. 37:8

"A wrathful man stirreth up strife: but he that is slow to anger appeaseth strife."   Prov. 15:18

"He that is slow to anger is better than the mighty; and he that ruleth his spirit than he that taketh a city."
Prov. 16:32

"The discretion of a man deferreth his anger; and it is his glory to pass over transgression."
Prov. 19:11

"But now ye also put off all these; anger, wrath, malice, blasphemy, filthy communication out of your mouth."   Col. 3:8

"For a bishop must be blameless, as the steward of God; not self willed; not soon angry, not given to wine, nor striker, not given to filthy lucre";   Titus 1:17

"For the wrath of man worketh not the righteousness of God."   Jas. 1:20

Apostasy: Desertion of one's faith, religion, party, or principles.
"Certain men, the children of Belial, are gone out from among you, and have withdrawn the inhabitants of their city, saying, Let us go and serve other gods, which ye have not known;   Deut. 13:13
"They on the rock are they, which, when they hear, receive the word with joy; and these have no root, which for a while believe, and in time of temptation fall away."
Luke 8:13

"From that time many of his disciples went back, and walked no more with him."   John 6:66

"For the time will come when they will not endure sound doctrine; but after their own lusts shall they heap to themselves teachers, having itching ears;
And they shall turn away their ears from the truth, and shall be turned unto fables."   2 Tim. 4:3-4

"Take heed, brethren, lest there be in any of you an evil heart of unbelief, in departing from the living God."   Heb. 3:12

"For it is impossible for those who were once enlightened, and have tasted of the heavenly gift, and were made partakers of the Holy Ghost,
And have tasted the good word of God, and the powers of the world to come,
If they shall fall away, to renew them again unto repentance; seeing they crucify to themselves the Son of God afresh, and put him to an open shame."
Heb. 6:4-6

"Ye therefore, beloved, seeing ye know these things before, beware lest ye also, being led away with the error of the wicked, fall from your own steadfastness."   2 Pet. 3:17

"They went out from us, but they were not of us; for if they had been of us, they would no doubt have continued with us: but they went out, that they might be made manifest that they were not all of us."   1 John 2:19

124

Chapter 14
When you think you've lost it . . .

Your Faith:

Sometimes it can happen. The reasons vary, but the results are the same.

You pray, but you really don't expect to have your prayers answered; you don't even *really pray;* you simply go through the motions. Perhaps it would be best expressed as a loss of hope, after all, "faith is the substance of things hoped for" (Heb. 11:1).

Your resulting loss of faith could have come about via a variety of different situations; like backsliding (when you expect God to continually keep you from sin), or financial problems, health problems, the death of a precious loved one, or worse yet, a child. Perhaps even one of your own children.

You realize that the God of all Comfort is supposed to be comforting you (that you might comfort others with the same comfort that you have received), but it just doesn't feel that way (2 Cor. 1:3-5). You feel that your prayer has been prayed in accordance with God's will (1 John 5:14-15), and you wonder why it hasn't been answered...

You must press on! In due time, God will indeed speak to you, if you have cultivated a personal relationship with Him through the person of Jesus Christ, and don't forget to read your Bible. God speaks to you continually through His Word.

In the meantime while you are waiting, repent for your loss of faith, and continue to thank God for the blessing that you are *still* receiving in the midst of your sorrow.

Your Gifts:

The Spirit divides His gifts "severally as He will" (1 Cor. 14:11).

If you don't use them, you'll lose them, and if you *misuse them, you'll lose them.

If you have been so blessed, remember that it is **NOT** you, but it is the Holy Spirit working through you! Stay humble. If you have indeed lost your gifts, you need to repent and ask forgiveness, and peradventure, God will return them to you again.

* You may want to read the account of the Jeffreys brothers; Stephen and George in the book *Pioneers of Faith,* written by Dr. Lester Sumrall, an d published by Harrison House Books in 1995.

Your "First Love:"

"Unto the angel of the church of Ephesus, write;

I know thy works, and thy labour, and thy patience, and how thou canst not bear them which are evil: and thou hast tried them which say they are apostles, and are not, and hast found them liars:

And hast born, and hast patience, and for my name's sake hast laboured, and hast not fainted.

Nevertheless I have somewhat against thee, because thou hast left thy first love.

Remember therefore from whence thou art fallen, and repent, and do the first works;

To him that overcometh will I give to eat of the tree of life, which is in the midst of the paradise of God."

Rev. 2: 1a, 2-4, 7b

Sometimes we forget how much on fire we were when we first met Jesus, and realized that we could be clean, new creatures in Him.

We start off on the narrow road exuberant, and

126

zealous, wanting to share the Gospel with every creature, wanting to testify about the goodness of God, wanting that the whole of mankind should desire nothing more of this life than to embrace Salvation, and serve the Lord.

There will be two distinct disappointments that we will have to face. The first one being: The world does not want Jesus!

"If the world hate you, ye know that it hated me before it hated you.

If ye were of the world, the world would love his own: but because ye are not of the world, but I have chosen you out of the world, therefore the world hateth you." John 15:18-19

The second disappointment comes when we join a church expecting everyone to be of the same mind as us: beacons of lights and blocks of salt for the unsaved (Matt. 5:13-14).

Unfortunately it doesn't happen that way. One of the greatest disappointments you will ever suffer, will be from the hands of your brethren, *The Churchfolk.*

There are many "lukewarm" Christians in the church, who want to do no more than warm their particular spot on their particular pew, Sunday after Sunday.

Their lack of zeal will eat away at your own if you let it. Not to mention the various un-Christian ways in which they hurt their brethren *"in the name of the Lord."*

You must fan the flames of your joy in the Lord continually. Remember always the pleasure that you found when your Salvation was new.

Stay in your WORD, and stay on your knees, this will renew your zeal daily.

"Look neither left nor right, but keep your eyes on Him," whom as Job said, "I shall see for myself, and mine eyes shall behold, and not another" (Job 19:27).

127

Chapter 15
The 'wife' in Relation to "the Bride of Christ"

"Wives, submit yourselves unto your own husbands, as unto the Lord.

For the husband is the head of the wife, even as Christ is the head of the church: and he is the savior of the body.

Therefore, as the church is subject unto Christ, so let wives be to their own husbands in everything.

Husbands, love your wives, even as Christ also loved the church, and gave himself for it;

For we are members of his body, of his flesh, and of his bones.

For this cause shall a man leave his father and mother, and shall be joined unto his wife, and they two shall be one flesh.

This is a great mystery: but I speak concerning Christ and the church."   Eph. 5:22-25,30-32

The institution of marriage, has, from the beginning been established to prepare us to become the "Brides of Christ."

In four separate places in the Bible, you will find that a man shall leave father and mother, and cleave unto his wife, and the two shall be one flesh (Gen. 2:24, Matt. 19:5, Mk. 10:7, Eph. 5:31).

For us as Christians, there should be no one else save Jesus. As a matter of fact, He tells us that whosoever will love

128

"father or mother, or son or daughter," more than Him is not worthy of Him (Matt. 10:37).

It is the same when we become a man's wife. He becomes first in our lives, followed by everyone else.

If we cannot be faithful, or loving, or honorable, or dedicated to our earthly spouse, how can we ever expect to be faithful, or loving, or honorable, or dedicated to our heavenly spouse?

Do you think that we can neglect Jesus and still go to heaven?

Do you think that we can commit adultery on Jesus and still go to heaven?

Do you think that we can half-step in any way, shape, or form, and still be considered the bride of Christ?

Do you think that we can divorce Jesus because some new, young stuff has caught our eye?

You need to realize that we as women who have entered into a marriage covenant here on earth, are really practicing for our eternal marriage that we will share with Christ forever in Heaven.

Chapter 16
If your name should be "Babylon"

If your name should be Babylon, then chances are you are quite a sumptuous and rich (as in chocolate mousse or roast ducking with cranberry gravy) creature.

Well bred and educated, (or giving the appearance of); beautiful to gaze upon, socially in demand, attending only the *best* affairs. You are cosmopolitan, well traveled, abreast of current events, possibly even fluent in another, or other languages.

Your home (and your car) will reflect your sumptuousness; fine artwork (some originals), sculptures, furnishings; beautiful clothes, furs and jewelry.

Everything in your world begins and ends with you. You are a lover of pleasures of *all* kinds; an obtainer of, dabbler in, and master of, some of the world's hidden knowledge.

The general historical description of Babylon is similar to the paragraphs above. Babylon was the capital of Babylonia. It was very cosmopolitan with great libraries and a vast collection of books (tablets). They were knowledgeable in many subjects including religion, medicine, mythology, the arts, geography, astronomy, the laws, poetry, fables, proverbs, divination, sorcery, necromancy, and magic.

The Bible also describes Babylon as being established by Nimrod (Gen. 10:10), whom Dr. Pink identifies as one of the Biblical antichrist types.

(See: Pink, Arthur W., Antichrist, published 1988, by Kregel Publications).

Babylon was the first society to rebel against God, and attempt not only to shape their own destiny, but to build a structure that reached to the heavens, possibly to depose or confront God.

Nevertheless, in this chapter, we are addressing the personage of "Babylon." The place of original apostasy; black arts, magic, necromancy, and every other dark and evil thing that lures mankind away from God, to seek the hidden knowledge that is forbidden them.

I had the occasion to meet a woman who was by no means the most beautiful woman that I had ever seen, and yet, I have really not seen another who is more beautiful. She possessed a certain "je ne c'est quois" as the French would say.

She was rich (not monetarily, but) in substance and character, and when you spent any amount of time in her presence, you were drawn to and *into* her being.

When I met her, she was a Born-again Christian, and it seemed that she possessed the same fire that Jeremiah had "shut up in his bones" (Jer. 20:9).

Although you could see the "light" of the Gospel, and feel the fire of her conviction when she spoke about Salvation, there always seemed to be something smoldering like a volcano about to erupt when she began to speak about the dark things that were an abomination to God.

I spent a goodly amount of time in her presence, and we spoke of many things. Finally I worked up enough nerve to ask her the question that had really been in the forefront of my mind since meeting her; "Who are you?"

She smiled a rather sad and knowing smile, and after some time of silence, she said, "*Now*, I am a child of the King, but before, if I had to use an all-inclusive name, my name was Babylon!"

"Well" I thought, "when are you just going to learn to mind your own business?" Sometimes we hear and learn things that we don't want to know! Yet, since "all things work together for good to them that love God, to them who are called according to his purpose" (Rom. 8:28), apparently, it was for God's purpose that I learned what I was about to learn from her that day...

She said, "For many years I served myself; I was narcissistic in my indulgences, and I was ever seeking to learn more and more about those things that I had later come to realize, were an abomination to God.

I dabbled in the Black Arts (possessing Tarot cards, wishing incense, fetishes, and literature). I thought of becoming a witch every now and then, (although never a Satanist, since I was only willing to serve myself). I considered spells, participated in a séance or two, and later on in my life, had access to the knowledge of being able to discern the time of a person's death - anyone at all.

Unbeknownst to me, the hand of God kept me always on the periphery of these things instead of becoming totally engrossed in them. There were many things I could have done, but for no reason that I could give, I never seemed to get around to doing them. Hallelujah!

I made myself the slave of a man for pleasure's sake, and made obeisance to other gods for the sake of continued pleasure, and the knowledge of pleasure, and for beauty's sake.

I took my pleasure in whatever way that I chose, and I gave nothing in return.

I regarded neither God nor man in my pursuit of pleasure, lawlessness, and debauchery of my own choosing.

I indulged myself in every earthly material good that I could afford, for I was much too independent to allow another to supply me with anything because I wanted to be indebted to no one.

I made my own rules and lived by them, and in my own eyes, *I was right!*

I prostituted the values instilled in me by my family for a position in the society of the educated elite (for they were not called 'New Agers' at that time). I believed that all paths led to God, and not that Jesus was the "Way, the Truth, and the Life" (John 14:6).

I seduced men and women alike, many of whom forsook

their own values to take a plunge into all that was evil. My darkness as it were, absorbed their light, and any good that was in them was forgotten. I was as beguiling as the serpent encountered by Eve in the Garden so long ago.

The funny thing is, that if you asked me if I thought I was a bad person, I would have told you no. After all, no one followed me by means of coercion.

I had immeasurable tenderness towards animal and plant life, but towards human life, I had only contempt. If I did not have a mother and a father to answer to, it is quite possible that I would have become a profession killer, for to me, humans were *the abomination*. They were sniveling, spineless, back stabbers, who lied, cheated, and hurt according to their whims and fancies. Predatory creatures who continually pressed their will and desires upon the weaker members of society.

I, on the other hand was much better than that, after all, I didn't inflict my will on anybody, I simply permeated the air around me with my Babylonish stink, and whosoever was captured by the aroma became ensnared like the unsuspecting fly that is drawn to the Venus Flytrap because of its intoxicating scent, only to be slowly consumed once it has landed. I too was a predator, but my prey were strictly those who considered themselves predators. Nothing gave me greater pleasure than to consume them mercilessly.

Somewhere along the line, I began to be contemptuous of those things that had once given me pleasure. I searched for new pleasures, but all that I found seemed to fall short of satisfaction.

I would like to tell you here that I sought God, but I did not..."

"But she that liveth in pleasure is dead while she liveth."   1 Tim. 5:6

I will end "Babylon's" story here, for after her encounter with God, just like God changed Abram's name, so it was that Babylon became a new creature, with a new name.

I hope that you will consider this story of "Babylon." There are many by that name in society today. They govern us, they create and vote upon our laws, they teach our children, they serve in our churches in the loftiest and the lowliest positions; their voice can be heard in the music we listen to, the books we read, the movies we see, and the shows we watch on television.

Babylon was, and will be an abomination to God. It is the site of Divine destruction, and the entire (material) world will mourn her:

"And he cried mightily with a loud strong voice, saying, Babylon the great is fallen, is fallen, and is become the habitation of devils, and the hold of every foul spirit, and a cage of every unclean and hateful bird.

For all nations have drunk of the wine of the wrath of her fornication, and the kings of the earth have committed fornication with her, and the merchants of the earth are waxed rich through the abundance of her delicacies.

How much she hath glorified herself, and lived deliciously, so much sorrow and torment give her: for she saith in her heart, I sit a queen, and am no widow, and shall see no sorrow.

Therefore shall her plagues come in one day, death, and mourning, and famine; and she shall be utterly burned with fire: for strong is the Lord God who judgeth her.

And the kings of the earth, who have committed fornication and lived deliciously with her, shall bewail her, and lament for her, when they shall see the smoke of her burning,

And the merchants of earth shall weep and mourn over her; for no man buyeth their merchandise anymore:

The merchandise of gold, and silver, and precious stones, and of pearls, and fine linen, and purple, and silk, and scarlet, and all thyine wood, and all manner of vessels of most precious wood, and of brass, and iron, and   marble,

134

And cinnamon and odours, and ointments, and frankincense, and wine, and oil, and fine flour, and wheat, and beasts, and sheep, and horses, and chariots, and slaves, and souls of men."   Rev. 18:2-3,7-9,11-14

If indeed your name should be "Babylon," take heed to the Scriptures and realize that God in His time will exact Divine judgment upon you!

*   *   *   *

If indeed your name should be "Babylon," remember, "For whosoever shall call upon the name of the Lord shall be saved."   Rom. 10:13

Chapter 17
Some of the more difficult 'wife' Scriptures
(Or, those pertaining to godly women)

"Let your women keep silence in the churches: for it is not permitted unto them to speak; but they are commanded to be under obedience, as also saith the law.
And if they will learn anything, let them ask their husbands at home: for it is a shame for women to speak in the church."
1 Cor. 14:34-35

"Let the women learn in silence with all subjection.
But I suffer a woman not to teach, nor usurp authority over the man, but to be in silence."
1Tim. 2:11-12

I had considered eliminating this chapter altogether, because of the controversial nature of the Scriptures involved. Nevertheless, because of their controversial nature, I am persuaded to proceed.

I have the occasion to evangelize those people that happen to stumble into my office unawares, as was the case with the young lady I am about to share with you.

She was a young woman in her early twenties whom I conversed with at the copy machine from time to time. Our common ground being my high-heeled shoes, and her desire to find a place to purchase some as high as mine.

However, one particular day she happened into my office. The conversation began innocently enough but, sometimes as you well know, out of nowhere, Jesus became

136

the topic of our conversation.

She considered herself a Christian even though she didn't accept Jesus as her own personal Savior, and believed that other religions also held the key to everlasting life in Heaven. She admitted that she really didn't *read* the Bible because its "sexist" verbiage completely turned her off.

Well, what could I say!

She proceeded to tell me that she felt the Bible should be non-gendered, (I wondered if she knew that there was already such a thing, and that some of the more *liberal* seminaries who shared the same sentiments as her were using it).

Nevertheless, I told her that the Original King James version of the Bible is the one that I not only recommended, but used as well, (sexist verbiage and all).

The reason I share this story with you is because there are many women out there who feel to some degree or another, just like her.

I see things happening in our churches today that are completely un-Biblical because one person or another does not agree with the Lord's way of expressing His desire for His people, and His church.

In regards to the above-mentioned Scriptures, some say that they were written by Paul and not God; others say the Scriptures pertained to the women in the church at Corinth, and/or the women of that time period in history, and not to the women of today.

I say that God says, "All scripture is... profitable for doctrine, for reproof, for correction, for instruction in righteousness" (2 Tim. 3:16).

So from that point of view is where my point of view must also come.

I will tell you honestly that when I began to read the Bible for myself, there were some things that I just didn't want to hear; however, since God said it, and I wanted to be with

God, and I wanted to please God, then I was going to have to "hear it, and do it."

From my experience as a minister and pastor's wife, I have to tell you, no one can disrupt a church service or a Bible study like a woman can.

Furthermore, in their rebellion, there has been much damage done to the Gospel and the church of Christ by women.

Women have been founders of damaging cults, and widespread New Age doctrines, having received "revelations" from God that were not in the Bible.

For your convenience, I will list just a few here:

Madame Helen Petrovna Blavatsky was a world famous medium, and co-founder of the Theosophy Movement.

Mary Baker Eddy founded the Christian Science Church, which still exists today.

Marilyn Ferguson is a prominent force and spokesperson for the Aquarian Conspiracy, which is a New Age doctrine.

Shirley McLaine promotes astral-projection, communing with demons (or spirit guides as they are now called), and the fact that *we* are gods.

There have been other women as well who even though they may not have founded a cult or religion, have done considerable damage to God's people, like *Betty J. Eadie*, who wrote the book Embraced by the Light (Gold Leaf Press, 1992).

If you've noticed now, Angelology has become very popular, and most of the angels that you see pictures of are women. As far as I can tell, there are no female angels in the Bible.

The feminist movement has infiltrated the Christian colleges and seminaries, and feminists are aligning themselves with minorities and homosexuals in hopes to give

138

their demands of equity credibility.

The last time I checked, homosexuality was a question of sexual preference, not ethnicity.

Nevertheless, I will now return to the mainstream of this chapter, which is, how we as church women should handle the above-mentioned Scriptures in a godly fashion; always being mindful that if we profess to love Jesus, then it is He who charges us on this wise; "If ye love me, keep my commandments" (John 14:15).

To substantiate this further, "In the beginning was the Word, and the Word was with God, and the Word was God" (John 1:2).

"And the Word was made flesh, and dwelt among us, (and we beheld his gory, the glory as of the only begotten of the Father) full of grace and truth" (John 1:14).

If you truly are a "church woman" after God's own heart, then you will accept what *thus sayeth the Lord* whether you like it, agree with it, can do it, or not.

Faith allows us to come to Jesus as we are, believing that He will make the necessary character changes that will allow us to be pleasing in His sight.

The Bible clearly states the position of a woman in regards to the church. She is not to be the Pastor, nor to have authority over men, nor to teach men.

She is to learn in subjugation and silence, and should she have any questions, she is to ask her husband (who is assumed to be a learned man since he is also assumed to be a godly man) in private (at home).

This has nothing to do with a woman being an evangelist, for technically speaking, we are all evangelists, called to preach the Gospel to "every creature" (Mk. 15:15), "that repentance and remission of sins should be preached... among all nations, beginning at Jerusalem" (John 21:47).

But be advised, all you evangelists who believe that you belong in the pulpit, (an evangelist is a soul winner), you

139

will never win a soul from the pulpit, you must go out to the highways and the hedges (Matt. 22:9-10, Luke 14:23).

The pulpit is really the spiritual trough, from which the Lord's under-shepherd feeds the Lord's sheep.

There are many reasons that we find women licensed as ministers and sitting in our pulpits today, and I am sorry to say, none of them are justified.

There are pastors who make bets with other pastors to see if they have enough power to license a woman and put her in their pulpit against the wishes of their particular denomination or conference. There are the trend setters and fad followers who go with whatever's popular.

There are weak pastors who bow to the demands of the female members of their congregation, or allow themselves to be blackmailed by the threat of their substantial (female) tithers to leave the church if their demands are not met, and so, they license women as ministers. Remember, "God loveth a cheerful giver" (2 Cor. 9:7) if their tithes are not given in the right spirit, they are of no use to you anyway.

There are pastor's wives who beguile their husbands into appointing them co-pastors of their particular church.

"For it came to pass, when Solomon was old that his *wives* turned away his heart after other gods: and his heart was not perfect with the LORD his God, as *was* the heart of David his father" (1 Kings 11:4).

There are women who become licensed through various liberal seminaries, who not only support women pastors, but also support other ways into Heaven in addition to Jesus, who plainly tells us that He is the only way (John 14:6).

There are women who as pastor's wives, are appointed to the pastorate because their husband may become incapacitated, or terminally ill. This way, the man ensures that *his* church will remain *his* church. This is a devilish idea because the church is God's church always and forever. "Their inward thought *is, that* their houses *shall continue* for ever, *and* their dwelling places to all generations; they call *their* lands after their own name" (Ps. 49:11).

And finally, for the unscrupulous, tabloids offer ordinations for various denominations for as little as $5.00.

There is no way that a woman can ever teach a man how to be a man. This is in no way a slight to the many woman who have raised daughters and sons without a husband/father.

Nevertheless, a man without the influence of a positive male figurehead is a totally different type of male than a male who has had the benefit of a strong, positive male role model.

Furthermore, it has been my experience, when you attend a woman's church, there a very few men to be found. The church is not just for women and children . . .

However, if a woman is assigned a duty in her church by her pastor, she is under the authority of her pastor. It is solely the pastor's responsibility to discern whether he has called her to perform a Biblically acceptable duty or not.

I imagine this particular chapter will meet with some disagreement; even so, I hope that it forces you to wonder if what I'm saying may be true.

In the event that you cannot bring yourself to agree with me, I have concluded with the following Scripture, which leaves no room for argument:

"For Adam was first formed, then Eve.
And Adam was not deceived, but the woman being
deceived was in the transgression. (emphasis mine)
1 Tim. 2:13-14

Therefore, the judgment of God has been rendered. There are many things that a woman can do in and for her church. As a matter of fact, there are some things that can *only* be done by a woman. You may wish to discuss with your pastor the inception of a women's ministry. There are many hurting women out there who need Christian care and compassion, and if they cannot look to the women of their church; their sisters in Christ, then to whom can they turn?

There is a book specifically addressing women's ministries called, *Women's Ministry Handbook* written by Carol Porter with Mike Hamel, and published by Victor Books, 1991.

Chapter 18
The Significance of the Armorbearer

In ancient times, no commander or officer going into battle would think of going without his armorbearer. Nelson's Illustrated Bible Dictionary presents this definition of the position of armorbearer:

"A servant who carries additional weapons for the Commander. Abimelech, Jonathan, and Joab had armorbearers. [A]morbearers were also responsible for killing enemies slain by their masters. After the enemy soldier was wounded with javelins or bow and arrows, the armorbearer finished the job by using clubs and swords."

Nelson's Illustrated Bible Dictionary, published by Thomas Nelson, 1986, pg. 770

This is a gruesome definition, but sometimes being a pastor or minister's wife can be a gruesome job.

As a pastor or minister's wife, you are your husband's armorbearer. It is your obligation, and duty as his "help meet", having been appointed him by God.

Since we are no longer living in ancient times, you may be wondering just what does a modern day *armorbearer* do?

Preserved for us in Scripture, we find:

"Then he (Abimelech) called hastily to his armourbearer, and said unto him, Draw thy sword, and slay me, that men say not of me, A woman slew him. And his young man thrust him through, and he died."

Judges 9:54

It may be that you need to help your husband die to

143

the "old man" and re-emerge as the "new" (Eph. 4:22-24). Many pastors' and ministers' wives are more than willing partners when they receive the material benefits of the ministry. However, it is unfortunate that some of these pastors' and ministers' wives cannot seem to be willing partners in the righteousness, dedication, and sacrifice that ministry entails.

Like God, Satan never slumbers nor sleeps. His time is limited, and he is continually on the prowl seeking "whom he may devour" (1 Pet. 5:8).

The church has become big business in this 21st Century. You have the emergence of "Faith Based Funding", which allows a religious institute to either partner with an existing agency, or create its own Community Development Corporation (CDC). This sounds like a great concept, because through the years, the church has had to rely solely on tithes and offerings to exist.

We now have pastors becoming licensed general contractors, and chief executive officers of their own corporations. Their days are spent wheeling and dealing, and thinking up ways to get and spend the Federal dollar.

They are too busy going to meetings to go to the hospitals and visit the sick and dying; they are too busy succeeding in the *world*, to ever be an effective tool against the *world*; they are too busy indulging in the very "concupiscence" (Col. 3:5) the Bible warns them to be wary of; and their wives are right there with them.

It is your duty and your calling to remind your husband that he is to crucify his flesh, and walk after those things which are spiritual (Gal. 5:24).

You must be willing to sacrifice for the glory of God, and for the blessing of His calling upon your life. The saints of old considered it a blessing to be called to sacrifice for the ministry of the Gospel of Jesus Christ (Rom. 8:17-18, 2 Tim. 2:12, Heb. 11:24-26, 1 Pet. 2:21).

From its foundation, the Church was ordained to survive on tithes and offerings. It's pretty sad when people will contribute to senior citizen apartments, or a learning center, or a grocery store, when they will not pay their tithes.

It is your job to bring your husband into remembrance as to what his calling is. Although, I have to be honest with you; there are some in the ministry that consider it a vocation, and have no intention of serving God. Perhaps it is even you and your husband...

There are also pastors who feel pressured and subsequently succumb to the idea that the Gospel is old fashioned, and it needs a little something to pep it up, and make it more palatable to a larger and more diverse audience. In the book of Colossians, in the second verse of the first chapter you will find these words, "To the saints and faithful brethren which are in Christ..."

I remember the first time I heard my husband teach on this small and over looked portion of Scripture; it was a profound lesson that I have always remembered.

It seems the church of old was much like the church of now, full of pseudo-saints, with a few "faithful brethren" in the mix. The "faithful brethren" are those who come to church to worship God in "spirit and in truth" (John 4:24), they are the ones that support the ministry not only with their tithes, but also with their time. They are the ones who believe that "all scripture is given by inspiration of God, and is profitable for doctrine..." (2 Tim. 3:16).

They are the ones who lovingly fulfill the Scriptural mandates, while faithfully watching and waiting for Christ's return. They are the ones who Paul says, "As it is written, For thy sake we are killed all the day long; we are accounted as sheep for the slaughter" (Rom. 8:36).

The "saints" are the ones who perceive church as a social gathering, and are more concerned with the number of initials behind their pastor's name, than with his godly

145

character.

They are the ones who are swayed by every "wind of doctrine" (Eph. 4:14) that comes their way. They want 'praise dancing' in the church because that's what other churches have; they want a mega-orchestra warm-up praise band in the church, because that's what other churches have, and are willing to spend hundreds and thousands of dollars to retain artists, when they are un-willing to extend the budget for Christian education, or subsidize ministries to the un-saved right in their own neighborhoods. It's pretty pitiful that people need to be psyched up before they can worship the very God that wakes them up, feeds them, clothes them, and keeps their family safe.

They are the ones that are more concerned with pomp and splendor than with godly truth and righteousness. They are the ones who are easily persuaded to believe those doctrines of men that promote the idea of the inerrancy of the Bible, because it's obvious their Bible isn't telling them what they want to hear, so it *must* be incorrect. They are the ones that believe that *perhaps* Jesus is the only way (John 14:6), but just in case there's another one, they keep their eyes and ears open.

As your husband's armorbearer, it is your job to follow him into spiritual battle, and aid him in those weak moments when his flesh would rise up and overcome him it if could. There may be times when you find that you will have to spiritually amputate some portion of willful flesh through intercessory prayer (and fasting).

You must encourage him to die to his flesh daily, and you must walk together with him along the "narrow way", wherein there is life found by only a *few* (Matt.7:14).

"And Jonathan climbed up upon his hands and upon his feet, and his armorbearer after him: and they fell before Jonathan; and his armorbearer slew after him."

1 Sam. 14:13

In Ephesians chapter six, beginning with the twelfth verse, Paul tells us that our fight is not against "flesh and blood, but against principalities, against powers, against the rulers of darkness of this world, against spiritual wickedness in high places" (Eph. 6:12).

If you continue on with this passage, you will find the articles that make up "the whole armor of God." As you can see, there is no piece of armor that covers the warrior's back.

It is your duty to follow your husband into these spiritual frays, and slay after him all manner of wickedness that would rise up against him.

Go to church with him! I know many of you feel that accompanying your husband to church each service is like stepping into a bed of poisonous vipers. Go anyway.

Pray, always covering him with the blood of our Lord and Savior, Jesus Christ. Anoint yourselves and your home (and your children) on a regular basis.

Don't be afraid of a good spiritual fight; "No weapon formed against thee shall prosper; and every tongue that *shall* rise against thee in judgment thou shalt condemn. This is the heritage of the servants of the LORD, and their righteousness is of me, saith the LORD" (Is. 54:17).

"For though we walk in the flesh, we do not war after the flesh:

(For the weapons of our warfare are not carnal, but mighty through God to the pulling down of strongholds;)"
2 Cor. 10:4

"And David came to Saul, and stood before him: and he loved him greatly; and he became his armourbearer."
1 Sam. 16:21
You must love your husband "greatly", as David loved Saul. You should share the vision that God has given him, and be willing to give your life for him.

Chapter 19
In Conclusion

"Finally my brethren, be strong in the Lord, and in the power of his might.

Wherefore, take unto you the whole armour of God, that ye may be able to withstand in the evil day, and having done all, to stand."   Eph. 6:10,13

There are many Christians who say they "have faith " in God, and yet their faith is never exercised. There are Christians who say that they've given this situation or that situation over to God, and yet they work feverishly to exercise their own will over their dilemma, hardly leaving room for God to accomplish anything on their behalf.

We can be sure that an "evil day" will come to all of us if we live long enough. It is how we "stand" in that "evil day" that will proclaim our victory in Jesus, or our defeat by our own flesh.

The Scripture plainly states, "having done *all* ..." Well, what does that mean to the Christian?

It should mean that we have the spirit of an overcomer.

The charge of being a pastor or minister's wife is not an easy one. There are many pastors that I have met who must labor alone because their wife was not up to that task of being a fellow laborer.

There are many women who marry clergymen for the wrong reasons. Instead of finding a life of ease, importance, and glamour, they find themselves toiling endlessly; giving of themselves when they feel that they have no more to give, and trying to live "holy," which seems to go against the grain of all the other things they want to do with their lives.

A pastor or minister's wife must stay in her Bible. She must pray continually, and truly, she must really have been called of God to her duty, for if she has not been called of God, she will not be able to "withstand in that evil day."

She must strengthen herself with the Word of God, for the Word of God is able to keep us unto the day that Jesus Himself returns to rapture His church.

"For as many as are led by the Spirit of God, they are the sons of God.

For ye have not received the spirit of bondage again, to fear; but ye have received the Spirit of adoption, whereby we cry, Abba, Father.

This Spirit itself beareth witness with our spirit, that we are the children of God:
And if children, then heirs; heirs of God, and joint-heirs with Christ; if so be that we suffer with him, that we may be also glorified together.

For I rekon that the sufferings of this present time are not worthy to be compared with the glory which shall be revealed in us." Rom. 8:14-18

"What shall we then say to these things? If God be for us, who can be against us?" Rom. 8:31

"Who shall separate us from the love of Christ? Shall tribulation, or distress, or persecution, or famine, or nakedness, or peril, or sword?

As it is written, For thy sake we are killed all the day long; we are accounted as sheep for the slaughter.

Nay, in all these things we are more than

conquerors through him that loved us.

For I am persuaded, that neither death, nor life, nor angels, nor principalities, nor powers, nor things present, nor things to come,

Nor height, nor depth, nor any other creature shall be able to separate us from the love of God, which is in Christ Jesus."   Rom. 8:35-39

"And the God of peace shall bruise Satan under your feet shortly. The grace of our Lord Jesus Christ be with you. Amen."   Rom. 16:20

"But as it is written, Eye hath not seen, nor ear heard, neither have entered into the heart of man, the things which God hath prepared for them that love him."
1 Cor. 2:9

"And let us not be weary in well doing: for in due season we shall reap, if we faint not."   Gal. 6:9

"Let no man deceive you with vain words: for because of these things cometh the wrath of God upon the children of disobedience.

Be ye not partakers with them."   Eph. 5:6-7

"Finally, my brethren, be strong in the Lord, and in the power of his might."   Eph. 6:10

"Not that I speak in respect of want: for I have learned, in whatsoever state I am, therewith to be content.

I know both how to be abased, and I know how to abound: every where and in all things I am instructed both to be full and to be hungry, both to abound and to suffer need.

I can do all things through Christ which

150

strengtheneth me."   Phil. 4:11-13

"But my God shall supply all your needs according to his riches in glory by Christ Jesus."
                                                        Phil. 4:19

"For God hath no given us the spirit of fear, but of power, and of love, and of a sound mind."   2 Tim.1:7

"It is a faithful saying: For if we be dead with him, we shall also live with him:
I we suffer, we shall also reign with him: if we deny him, he also will deny us":   2 Tim. 2:11

"Yea, and all that will live godly in Christ Jesus shall suffer persecution."   2 Tim. 3:12

"For yet a little while, and he that shall come will come, and will not tarry.
Now the just shall live by faith: but if any man draw back, my soul shall have no pleasure in him.
But we are not of them who draw back unto perdition; but of them that believe to the saving of the soul."   Heb. 10:37-39

"Blessed is the man that endureth temptation: for when he is tried, he shall receive the crown of life, which the Lord hath promised to them that love him."
                                                        Jas. 1:12

And finally;

"If ye then be risen with Christ, seek those things which are above, where Christ sitteth on the right hand of God.
Set your affection on things above, not on things on the earth.

And whatsoever ye do in word or deed, do all in the name of the Lord Jesus, giving thanks to God and the Father by Him."   Col. 3:1-2, 17

Appendix A
Will the real Christian(s) Please Stand Up!

"A certain man had two sons; and he came to the first, and said, Son, go work to day in my vineyard.

He answered and said, I will not: but afterward he repented, and went.

And he came to the second, and said likewise. And he answered and said, I go sir: and went not.

Whether of them twain did the will of his father?"

Matt. 21:28-31

Many times we will see a Christian with an *attitude*, and we instantly judge that person. We compare them to someone else that we may know who appears to be pleasant, and kind, and hospitable, etc., never realizing that the person we find to be so unpleasant is actually a "doer of the word," and not just a "hearer."

I have met a lot of pleasant Christians in my experiences who seem to be so congenial, and certainly would love to do *something* for you in the name of the Lord; some of them even promise to do something for you, but it seems that whatever the something is that you ask them for, it's always the exception to what they are able do.

My husband and I had a ministry for a while in which we took in women who were drug addicts, and usually ex-cons as well. There were times when we would encounter some of our more mainstream Christian associates, who

153

assured us that indeed there was definitely a *need* for what we were doing, but we would have to think they were "crazy" if we expected them to take "these (kind of) people into *their* home."

I have to admit, sometimes I thought we were crazy too, but we were doing what God told us to do. Speaking for myself, there were times that I was less pleasant than I should have been.

When we first started our church, we did so in our home. It was the norm for street people to show up at our house on Sunday early, so that if they needed a shower and a change of clothes, they would be able to do that, and be ready for the service on time.

I can remember a particular Sunday a young lady named Lisa appeared at our door.

No one cared for Lisa because among other things, Lisa was a thief. Nevertheless, there were moments that I felt more compassion for Lisa than I should have, and I would let her into the house for a few minutes. I had had that moment earlier in the week, and Lisa had stolen $140 dollars worth of food stamps, which the boarders had chipped in for groceries.

Needless to say, I was thoroughly disgusted with Lisa for being such a sleaze, and even more disgusted with myself for being so naive.

As I sat in my kitchen early that Sunday morning, I thought about Lisa, and wondered if I would see her again.

The Lord spoke to me, and let me know that when the people got to us, it was because they had nowhere else to go, so I'd be seeing Lisa again.

A few minutes later the house seemed to be in a tizzy. Someone came running to the kitchen to tell me, "Lisa's here, should we send her away?"

"No" I said, "just send her in here where I can have a little talk with her."

I proceeded to let Lisa know that I knew she was the

one who had stolen from us earlier in the week. With a lot of hemming and hawing, she admitted it. "Whew" I thought, "that makes me feel better."

Now we could get onto the real reason she had come, the change of clothes and the service.

Well, I supplied her with a towel, and the dress that she normally wore when she came to church. However, this particular morning, Lisa was going to try my Christian patience. Before getting in the shower, she said, "do you have a curling iron I could use?" I didn't, but one of the other girls did-no problem.

When she got out of the shower, my daughter came downstairs and said, "Lisa wants you," well I thought, "what could she want now?"

She met me at the top of the stairs; "I need a bra!"

My mind reached out and punched her right in the nose, however, my lips said, "wait right here."

I ran in my room, shut the door, started tossing about my underwear drawer, and fussing to God . . . "Lord," I said, "I can't believe you have me in here looking for a bra! You know this _____ already robbed us this week, I've given her a shower, clothes, she's done her hair, and now you want me to give her a *BRASSIERE* too." As the last word hissed from between my lips, I laid hands on a bra. With bra in hand, seething like a cauldron about to boil over, I reached my bedroom door. Miraculously, between the time my hand touched the door knob, until the time it opened and she saw my face, a transformation had taken place. I opened the door, and with a smile on my face, I said, "here you go Honey."

I would tell you that I couldn't believe it, but when it comes to God making instant attitude adjustments for me, I know that He is able to do "exceeding abundantly above all that we ask or think..." (Eph. 3:20).

Don't always judge according to pleasantness. Judge with your heart, according to your heart.

Jesus wasn't always pleasant, but He was reliable, honest, compassionate, loving, and "real."

*   *   *   *

"Woe unto you scribes and Pharisees, hypocrites! For ye are like unto white sepulchres, which indeed appear beautiful outward, but are within full of dead men's bones, and of all uncleanness.

Even so ye also outwardly appear righteous unto men, but within ye are full of hypocrisy and iniquity."

Matt. 23:27-28

Hypocrite: *One who acts a false part or makes false professions; the feigning to be what one is not.*

I know and have known a goodly number of Christian hypocrites, and I believe that out of the whole group of prejudiced, puffed-up, fornicating; self-worshiping; covetous; arrogant; self-serving; "do as I say/not as I do" Christians, hypocrites are the worse. You see, hypocrisy encompasses all of the above and then some. You may consider this a harsh judgment, but the very moment you profess godliness, and you live worldliness, you become a hypocrite.

The Pharisees professed godliness, but they were living worldliness. They were God's men in the field, but when they thought Jesus was moving in on their thing, instead of acknowledging what the Scriptures said about the Messiah, they became envious and sought to kill him.

If I had to acknowledge one weak area in my being a Christian, it would be dealing with hypocrites. I absolutely cannot stomach them even for a second.

One of my Christian friends was laughing at me one day because I was sharing with her how abominable it is for me to listen to people who know that they are living ungodly lives, stand up in church and "give honor to God who is first in their life … " I wonder if God is first in their life when they are sitting on the barstool, or cheating on their taxes, or displacing some senior citizen, and taking their house for taxes instead of paying the taxes off for them. I wonder if God is first in their life when they tell their wife they'll be home late for dinner, and then go out with their girlfriend. I wonder if God is first in their life when they are getting high, or when they refuse to acknowledge their illegitimate child or children. I wonder if God is first in their life when they proposition every man or woman in the church for sex. I wonder if God is first in their life when they refuse to preach about sin from their pulpit because it may discourage the larger contributors from giving. I wonder if God is first in their life when they are making a scene because they are not singing that day's solo in the choir.

My friend told me I just "couldn't stand a hypocrite;" I told her she was right, "pray for me."

I have another friend that called me 'Jonah' when I told her I didn't know what God was waiting for, our town was so sinful I couldn't understand why He just didn't rain down fire and brimstone as in the days of Sodom and Gomorrah. She laughed and told me she would try never to get on a boat with me, but if she ended up on a boat with me, as soon as the storm arose she was going to throw me overboard, no questions asked. I love my friends. They make me laugh at myself.

I am extremely serious about what the Bible says. I have a 'front line' mentality, and find myself always to be in 'warrior' mode. Sometimes I need to loosen up and laugh a little; my friends make that possible for me. "God Bless them always. Amen."

*   *   *   *

"Two men went up into the temple to pray; the one

157

a Pharisee, and the other a publican.

The Pharisee stood and prayed thus with himself, God, I thank thee, that I am not as other men are, extortioners, unjust, adulterers, or even as this publican.

I fast twice in the week, I give tithes of all that I possess.

And the publican, standing afar off, would not lift up so much as his eyes unto Heaven, but smote his breast, saying, God be merciful to me a sinner.

I tell you, this man went down to his house justified rather than the other: for every one that exalteth himself shall be abased; and he that humbleth himself shall be exalted."   Luke 18:10-14

Are you familiar with the phrase "humbly superior." It is one of those phrases that pops up in Christian conversation from time to time.

At first it sounds kind of nice, but the more you consider it, the more you paint a mental picture of the Pharisee and the Publican, and guess which one *you* are!?

Yes I know that we 'saved' sinners are not like the *other* sinners, and in most cases (but not all cases), we no longer fornicate, lie, commit adultery, worship idols, practice any type of objectionable occult methods of discernment (like reading our daily horoscope), we never bear false witness, nor are we busybodies or tattlers. We're just as "holy" as we want to be . . .

Excuse me! My Bible tells me that " . . . all our "righteousnesses *are* as filthy rags . . . " (Is. 64:6), and that *"all* have sinned and come short of the glory of God" (Rom. 3:23).

I had a guy tell me one day that churches should have assigned seating, with the most heinous sinners relegated to the back. Can you believe it! Personally, I think they should have the seats closest to the pulpit (just kidding).

As we are being transformed by the renewing of our

158

minds, it is important to realize that our sins will change. And if we are really being transformed, we will find James 4:17 extremely significant in our lives: "Therefore, to him that knoweth to do good, and doeth it not, to him it is sin."

The devil's greatest area of assault is the battlefield of our minds (which includes our ego), he may not be able to get us to fornicate anymore, or to use foul language, but he can get us to feel "humbly superior" to our fellow stumbling, sinning, brothers and sisters in Christ. He can get us to feel intellectually superior because we can memorize Scriptures better, or read aloud better, or have one of those coveted degrees that now a days seems to be how the church evaluates their men (and women) of God. Possibly God has blessed you to be able to remember where things are in the Bible, so that people come to you often to find this or that Scripture. Perhaps, He has even blessed you with a degree. Don't forget where it came from. (I know a female minister whose only concern is letting people know the name of the seminary she graduated from). She has even gone so far as to suggest that when the church has Friends and Family Day, all of the graduates from *her* Alma Mater should be seated together. Do you think God has special categories in Heaven for Seminarians, as opposed to those who were called "according to His purpose?" (Rom. 8:28).

I believe that Job expresses it best when he says, "the LORD gave and the LORD hath taken away, blessed be the name of the LORD" (Job 1:21). The same way you got it, is the same way you can lose it!

I suggest that you check yourself regularly just in case some unwanted, fleshly baggage has attached itself to you. (Reread chapter 13, and make a list of the emergencies; put them somewhere that you will see them occasionally if not more, just to remind yourself of how "not to be").

It is easy to feel superior because by human standards we can always find *someone* to be superior to. No one but you knows what you were when God found you and made you a new creature. Many of us look back, and remembering our old selves, we are singularly elated not to be that person anymore; which is okay.

Instead of feeling superior, we need to feel grateful; chosen (for we could do nothing to save ourselves [Eph. 2:8]), and humbly submissive to God's word (all of it), and God's will.

*   *   *   *

"But a certain man named Ananias, with Sapphira his wife, sold a possession,

And kept back part of the price, his wife also being privy to it, and brought a certain part, and laid it at the Apostles' feet.

But Peter said, Ananias, why hath Satan filled thine heart to lie to the Holy Ghost, and to keep back part of the price of the land?

Whiles it remained, was it not thine own? And after it was sold, was it not in thine own power? why hast thou conceived this thing in thine heart? thou hast not lied unto men, but unto God.

And Ananias hearing these words fell down, and gave up the ghost: and great fear came on all them that heard these things.

And the young men arose, wound him up, and carried him out, and buried him.

And it was about the space of three hours after, when his wife, not knowing what was done, came in.

And Peter answered unto her, Tell me whether ye sold the land for so much? And she said, Yea, for so much.

Then Peter said unto her, How is it that ye have agreed together to tempt the Spirit of the Lord? behold,

160

the feet of them which have buried thy husband are at the door, and shall carry thee out.

Then fell she down straightway at his feet, and yielded up the ghost: and the young men came in, and found her dead, and carrying her forth, buried her by her husband." Acts 5:1-10

Let me ask you something? Do you know of any Christian that has ever cheated the Church?

When we first started in the ministry, my husband and I attended a very large, influential church.

Whenever a person made a donation to the church, they would insist the ushers take a slip immediately to the pulpit so a minister could announce their "very generous donation." If they were lucky, the usher made it to the pulpit while the service was still being broadcast on the local radio station.

There were some who would put an exorbitant figure on the outside of their tithes and offering envelope, only for the people in the finance office to discover that the envelope was empty.

I know of a young minister who would borrow from the church regularly, always promising to pay back his debt; to this day, I don't think he has given them one penny towards what they loaned him.

There was a gentleman that joined our church, and he was always suggesting different programs we should institute, and various functions we should have.

He was waiting for a large settlement, and promised that as soon as he got his money, he would make a generous donation to the church.

His settlement finally came. He invited the whole church to his house for a bar-b-que on his new deck, and to watch the football game on his new big-screen television. He never did contribute.

There are many fraudulent "Christians" not unlike Annanias and Sapphira, who talk godly giving, but who have no intention of ever practicing godly giving, they simply want the other Christians to think they are giving in the spirit of godliness.

For some reason that I will never be able to comprehend, people who have no problem fooling other people, think they are also fooling God.

"The heart is deceitful above all things, and desperately wicked: who can know it?

I the Lord search the heart, I try the reins, even to give every man according to his ways, and according to the fruits of his doings" (Jer. 17:9-10).

*   *   *   *

"This know also, that in the last days perilous times shall come.

For men shall be lovers of their own selves, covetous, boasters, proud, blasphemers, disobedient to parents, unthankful, unholy,

Without natural affection, trucebeakers, false accusers, incontinent, fierce, despisers of those that are good,

Traitors, heady, highminded, lovers of pleasures more than lovers of God:

Having a form of godliness, but denying the power thereof: from such turn away.

For of this sort are they which creep into houses, and lead captive silly women laden with sins, led away with diverse lusts,

Ever learning, and never able to come to the knowledge of the truth.

Now as Jannes and Jambres withstood Moses, so do these also resist the truth: men of corrupt minds,

reprobate concerning the faith." 2 Tim. 3:1-8

The Apostle Paul wrote these words to Timothy concerning the Church and apostasy. For even then, apostasy was infiltrating the Christian churches.

As we look about us, on a daily basis we can see that we are living in the last days as they are described in our Bibles. If we took each example given to us, we find that most of the predictions have already come to pass, with the remaining ones visible to us on the future's horizon.

The most significant thing about this portion of Scripture is not the frightening description of the apostates, but rather, the most significant thing is that Paul is addressing this Scripture to the apostates *already* in the church!

And we still have them, don't we!

People who love themselves more than God; pastors and ministers and their wives, who love themselves more than God; deacons and choir members who loves themselves more than God; people sitting in the pews, who love themselves more than God. They adorn themselves like peacocks, and surround themselves with all sorts of finery in the name of the Lord; but don't ever *need* anything from them, because if what you need won't benefit their cause, they can't help you.

We have members of congregations (including pastors and ministers) who are covetous of what their neighbor has.

I know a Pastor that had to have his church build him a mansion outside of town, because another church had built a mansion for their pastor, and he wanted one too.

There are a lot of braggarts in the church. Always wanting you to know how much they tithe, how smart their children are, what good jobs they have... but they never remember where their blessings came from. I know church people who still quote "the Lord helps those that help them selves," then they proceed to help themselves to everything they can possibly get. (By the way, I have never read that quotation in my Bible).

I know preachers that, after God has blessed them with a powerful message, and many come forward, instead of being grateful, they brag to their minister friends how *they* had the people rolling in the aisles.

Church folk are proud too. It's hard to find a humble soul in the entire body sometimes.

Long ago, when my husband and I were first beginning in the ministry, a particular Bishop befriended us.

One night, he invited us over to talk to my husband about joining a conference that he was beginning.

It came up in the conversation that another Bishop was planning to start his own conference as well.

My husband asked him why didn't he just join this other Bishop's conference...

Well, this poor man swelled up like a puffer fish. I though for sure he was going to burst any second.

He looked at my husband, and he told him, "I know the first shall be last and the last first, but I'm not following behind any man..."

There are a lot of blaspheming Christians in the church. Blasphemy isn't just using God's name in vain, but it encompasses the use of Jesus' name as well, and it is using their names in an impious, irreverent manner. Not only do the Christians blaspheme, we watch shows on television that blaspheme God, and we wonder what is wrong with our children, and why they are so disobedient, and disrespectful of the things of God.

The Scripture says that "they" will be disobedient to parents, but I have found that as long as I hold my Christian ground, and have set a Christian foundation under my child that their disobedience is short lived.

The Scripture further states that Christians will be "unthankful and unholy, and with out natural affections."

I know there are many both in and out of the pulpits,

and in seminaries that are unthankful; they feel that everything they've gotten, and everywhere they've gone is because of their own selves.

They live unholy lives in fornication, and lust, and debauchery. They are consumed with their own value and importance, and they live for the acclaim of others.

Many of them are practicing 'alternative' lifestyles, which is bad enough, but now there are churches that condone these lifestyles and attribute to them a Biblical basis for acceptance.

They make promises and agreements that they do not intend to keep; they accuse their fellow Christians falsely for their own gain, and are inconsistent in their Christian walk.

There was a church that we knew of that held 'recovery' Bible studies for recovering addicts and alcoholics. There was one young man in particular who attended faithfully these studies. One day he didn't show up, and the Pastor became worried. He went to the young man's home and asked him what happened to cause him to stop attending the studies.

He said, "Pastor, last week I went to the crack house to get high. The minister who conducts your recovery Bible study was there too. He gave me ten dollars not to mention he was there..."

Christians are "fierce" these days. Have you ever been in a meeting where a disagreement erupts, and threats start flying, or seen one of you fellow laborers of the cross out in the street cussing someone out, or threatening to thrash them within an inch of their lives?

Have you ever been in church when a fist-fight erupts between preachers, or between their wives and "the other woman?"

I have also noticed that if there is a true Christian in the congregation, there will always be critics despising them for their love of God's righteousness.

There are many pastors and ministers who "sell out," and instead of bringing them into remembrance, their wives are right there with their hands outstretched to make sure they get their share.

I know a pastor that was called to a church. He was such a dynamic preacher that the Church grew tremendously. It grew so large that he convinced the congregation to build a bigger church. They have just completed a church that will seat seven thousand people.

This pastor also has political designs. Even though his church is very large now, it does not sit in the location best suited to run for public office (and this guy wants to be Governor). Well, as luck would have it, the pastor of the church best suited for this pastor's run for public office died recently.

The pastor with the political ambitions applied for the pastorate of the politically strategic church, and is willing to let his flock suffer, not to mention the huge investment they made in building a larger building, all to satisfy his fleshly lust of ambition. The question becomes, who will he then serve? The Bible clearly states, "No man can serve two masters: for either he will hold to the one and love the other; or else he will hold to the one, and despise the other. Ye cannot serve God and mammon" (Matt. 6:24). If he is not careful, he will find himself a traitor to God's cause, having left his "first estate" not unlike the angels mentioned in Jude.

Without being repetitious, I say to you that we have become as Christians, "heady, high-minded, and lovers of pleasures more than lovers of God." That is so frightening. Not because of the wrath of God, but because I remember the moment that I met God; I remember the moment that He set me free; I remember the moment that He first spoke to me, and I remember the moment that I discovered the power I had in Him and through Him. It frightens me that we can so easily forget who saved our lives and gave us life.

166

We come now to my favorite portion of this particular scripture: "having a form of godliness but denying the power thereof..." (vs. 5).

There are many Christians; pastors and ministers included, who go through the motions of Christianity, but they expect no miracles, and they get none.

I have encountered ministers who believe that Satan is merely a metaphor for bad things. They would never dream of rebuking him as Jesus did, or casting demons out of people (as Jesus did).

They wouldn't dream of anointing with oil.

They don't believe the Gifts of the Spirit are available to the Saints today.

They don't even believe in helping another minister get started, or passing their ministry on. They would take it jealously to the grave with them if they could.

They pray, but they don't really expect an answer; certainly not an audible answer from God (John 10:27).

There are many Christians, pastors and ministers alike who have never encountered the presence of the Holy Spirit.

The preachers preach every Sunday from a sermon idea derived from their own mind, with a message that is solely theirs, and they wonder what is wrong with their congregation, and why their church is lukewarm.

They are "ever learning, and never able to come to the knowledge of the truth" (vs. 7).

There are many, like Jannes and Jambres who put on man made spectacles, (and some that are a little more sophisticated, that produce demon made spectacles) because they are unaware that Jesus is still the worker of miracles.

Recently some friends of ours traveled a considerable distance to one of these stadium healing extravaganzas. Fortunately or unfortunately (it all depends on how you look at it), they arrived a little too early. They came upon the "healer's" staff members as they coached their wheel chair

167

victims/miracle heal*ees* in the art of jumping out of the chair, and announcing convincingly, "I'm healed."

Timothy further says that "they" will resist the truth (vs. 8). Once, we were members of a church that considered itself "progressive." Someone talked the Pastor into letting a woman who specialized in meditation hold a few sessions for the members of the congregation during the week.

Because my husband was an associate minister there during this time, he was required to attend. He asked if I would accompany him. I didn't really want to, but I went anyway. I'm glad I did.

At the beginning of the session, the facilitator assured us that we were going to practice "godly" meditation. I didn't want to tell her, but I wasn't planning on practicing *any* meditation.

The first thing she did was to tell us that we were going to breathe, and as we inhaled and exhaled, we would be breathing in the "Holy Spirit." Well, I never read that the Holy Spirit could be inhaled and exhaled at will.

Then she instructed the people to close their eyes, and go to a place in their mind, and see what they see; ie: *visualization.* At the end of the exercise, she said, "okay, you can come back now."

I and my husband's experience was in spiritual warfare. When the woman said we were going to breathe in and out the Holy Spirit, I knew already that she was the enemy; as our eyes met, I knew that she knew, that I knew she was the enemy too.

During the duration of her exercise, my husband and I did not close our eyes; we held hands and prayed continually until it was over.

When she signaled everyone to "come back," I wondered how many of them actually "went somewhere," for we were praying fervently they would not.

Sometimes I hate to say it, but Christians aren't

exactly the smartest people in the world. They are so anxious to have an experience bigger and better than their fellow Christians that they soon find themselves caught up and blown by every wind of doctrine (false) that comes their way (Eph. 4:14).

My husband went to the pastor and told him about this woman. He told him about the Bible's definition of meditation (which is the total antithesis of what the meditation specialists teach), and he told him about the ungodliness of the situation. The pastor's reply was to say that she must have been mistaken regarding her reference to the Holy Ghost, and he would have a little talk with her. I can remember sitting there thinking "what can he possibly tell the devil, and how can he even think to match wits with the covering cherub (Eze. 28:14)?"

This pastor was blinded by his own arrogance, and was resisting the truth.

This Scripture gives a warning to stay away from these types of Christians. It further warns that these are the types that "lead captive, silly women laden with sins, led away with their own lusts" (vs. 6).

I believe the term "silly women" to be a metaphor for all of the foolish who are lead astray in like manor.

Sometimes we think more highly of ourselves than we ought. We fail to realize that we must continually be in the Truth; read the Truth, walk in the Truth, and hold fast to the Holy Spirit, who will teach us in all Truth, in order that we may not stray from the Truth and become a 'silly woman' being led away by our own desire for grandeur, hidden knowledge, spiritual spectacles, and worldly religions.

"So do these resist the truth, men of corrupt minds, reprobate concerning the faith" (vs. 8).

A lot of times we look for the obvious, when it is the not-so-obvious that we are in danger of.

We consider the 'Jim Jones' and the 'David Koreshes'

when we think of "men of corrupt minds, reprobate concerning the faith," but I challenge you today to truly grasp what Paul is trying to tell us here.

The word reprobate means (among other things), " One lost to all sense of duty or decency."

This would include the pastor who is unscrupulous in his work ethic, coveting power and money instead of the "good name" described in Proverbs 22:1. It would include the pastor with the wife and girlfriend; the pastor who likes to give special attention to the 'little boys'; the alcoholic pastor, the drug using pastor, the pastor with illegitimate children by various women in the congregation. It includes the pastor that preaches the funeral of one "Hell bound," but doesn't want to offend, so he lies and says they are heaven bound. The Bible says "preach the word; be instant, in season, out of season; reprove, rebuke, exhort with all longsuffering and doctrine" (2 Tim. 4:2).

This would certainly incorporate the deacon who would rather give the church monies to the pastor than to make sure God's church is being sustained, and the deacon who will turn a blind eye to his pastor's philandering. The Word says, "the wages of sin is death" (Rom. 6:23).

This also includes Scripture twisters, those who tempt the Lord with all types of craziness (like drinking poison because the Bible says, "if they drink any deadly thing, it shall not hurt them" (Mk. 16:18). The Bible does not teach us to tempt God with His word. When we do that, we are no different than Satan in the Wilderness, when he tempted Jesus with the twisted word of God (Matt. 4:1-11, Mk. 1:12-13, Luke 4:1-13).

I sincerely ask you to ask God to open your spiritual eyes, that you might see. If I continued with my list, it would be endless, and it is far more beneficial for you, if you see for yourself, and not just have my word on the matter.

We together must watch and wait, and it is important

that we all be spiritually equipped to do so.

I hope that with these few examples you will be able to discern the 'real' Christians from the counterfeits.

Appendix B
Numbers in Scripture

Author's note: The information in this section has been taken from the pages of the book, NUMBER IN SCRIPTURE, written by E.W. Bullinger, and published by Kregel Publications, 1967. It is only a small extraction from the whole and should be treated as such. This small extraction in no wise does justice to the whole of Bullinger's great work, which I highly recommend.

The purpose of this appendix is to broaden the readers perception of those things that we may consider coincidental or inconsequential; and to make the reader aware of the awesomeness of the True and Living God, whose depth and breadth and height we cannot begin to fathom.

*Gematria(pg. 48) = numbers formed by the letters of the words. This is the use of letters of the alphabet instead of figures. Arabic numerals being a comparatively modern invention were not, of course known to, and could not have been used by, the more ancient nations. (This pertains to the Hebrew and Greek alphabets).

ONE: (pgs. 50,51)
There can be no doubt as to the significance of this primary number. In all languages it is the symbol of *unity*. As a cardinal number it denotes *unity*; as an ordinal number it denotes *primacy*. Unity being indivisible, and not made up of other numbers, is therefore independent of all others, and is the source of all others. So with the Deity. The great first cause is independent of all. All stand in need of Him, and He needs no assistance from any.

"One" excludes all difference, for there is no second with which it can either harmonize or conflict.

When it is written: "Hear, O Israel, the Lord thy God is one Lord," it does not deny the Doctrine of the Trinity, but it excludes absolutely *another* Lord: it excludes, therefore, all idolatry.

Hence the First Commandment declares: Thou shalt have no other gods . . . " (Ex. 20:3).

It asserts that there is in God a *sufficiency* which needs no other; and an *independence* which admits no other.

It marks the *beginning*. We must begin with God. All our words and works must be characterized by the *first* words of the Bible: "In the beginning GOD." Nothing is right that does not begin with Him. "God first" is the voice of the scripture. "Seek ye first the kingdom of God and His righteousness; and all these things shall be added unto you" (Matt. 6:33) is the testimony of Christ. "God first" is the great proclamation. The angels sang: "Glory to God in the highest." This was the beginning of their song. And it was after this that they sang of "good-will" towards man. This, too, must be the great principle governing all our testimony and our work. We cannot give "glory to God" without doing good to men. And there is no real good-will for men which does not spring from a desire to glorify God.

Man's ways and thoughts are the opposite of God's. God says, "Seek *first*." *Man* says, "Take care of number one." He is in his own eyes this "number one," and his great aim is to be independent of God.

Independence, in God is His glory. Independence in man, is his sin and rebellion, and shame.

In the Word of God, therefore, God is *first*, and before all.

"Hearken unto Me, O, Jacob, and Israel My called;
I am He; I am the first, I also am the last.
Mine hand also hath laid the foundation of the earth,

173

And my right hand hath spanned the heavens."

Isaiah 48:12-13

"Before Me there was no God formed,
Neither shall there be after Me.
I, even I, am the Lord;
And beside Me there is no Savior."

Isaiah 43:10-11

"I am the Alpha and Omega,
The first and the last."

Rev. 1:11, 17, 2:8, 22:13

TWO: (pgs. 92,93,104,105)

We now come to the spiritual significance of the number two. We have seen that *One* excludes all difference, and denotes that which is sovereign. But two affirms that there is a difference-there is *another*; while One affirms that there is not another!

This difference may be for good or evil.

It is the first number by which we can *divide* another, and therefore in all its uses we may trace this fundamental idea of *division* or *difference*.

The *two* may be, though different in character, yet one as to testimony and friendship. The second that comes in may be for help and deliverance. But alas! Where man is concerned, this number testifies of his fall, for it more often denotes that difference which implies *opposition*, *enmity*, and *oppression*.

Take the *second* statement in the Bible. The first is-Gen. 1:1 "In the beginning God created the heaven and the earth." The second is "And the earth was (or rather *became*) without form and void." Here the first speaks of perfection and of order. The *second* of ruin and desolation, which came to pass at some time, and in some way, and for some reason which are not revealed.

But we have seen that where there are two, though

there is still *difference*, this difference may be in a good sense. It may be for oppression or hindrance, or it may be for association and mutual help.

Especially does it mark that "other," the Savior and mighty deliverer, spoken of in Ps. 89:19: "I have laid help on one that is mighty." The *second* person of the Trinity partook of two natures-perfect God and perfect man. Perfect man indeed, but oh, how *different!*

Two *testimonies* may be *different*, but yet one may support, strengthen, and corroborate the other. Jesus said; "The testimony of two men is true. I am the one that bear witness of myself, and the father that sent me beareth witness of me" (John 8:17-18). And it is written in the Law: "At the mouth of two witnesses, or three witnesses," shall the matter be established (Num. 35:30; Deut. 17:6, 19:15; Matt. 18:16; 2 Cor. 13:1; 1Tim. 5:19; Heb. 10:28). The whole law itself hung on "two commandments" (Matt. 22:40).

THREE: (pgs.107, 108,111,116)

We come to the first geometrical figure. Hence *three* is the symbol of the *cube*- the simplest form of solid figure. *Three* therefore stands for that which is *solid, real, substantial, complete,* and *entire*. All things that are specially complete are stamped with the number three.

When we come to the Scriptures, this completion becomes *Divine*, and marks Divine completeness or perfection.

Three is the first of four perfect numbers.
Three denotes *Divine* perfection;
Seven denotes *spiritual* perfection;
Ten denotes *ordinal* perfection; and
Twelve denotes *governmental* perfection.

Three is the number associated with the Godhead, for

there are "three persons in one God."

"The third day"was the day on which the earth was caused to rise up out of the water, symbolical of that resurrection life which we have in Christ, and in which alone we can worship, or serve, or do any "good works."

Hence *three* is the number of resurrection, for it was on the *third* day that Jesus rose from the dead. It was the *third* day on which Jesus was "perfected" (Luke 13:32). It was at the *third* hour He was crucified; and it was for *three* hours (from the 6th to the 9th) that darkness shrouded the Divine Sufferer and Redeemer.

The Three-fold nature of man: Spirit, and Soul, and Body, the man consisting of neither separately, but of the whole three together.

FOUR: (pgs.123,127)

Now the number *four* is made up of three and one (3+1=4), and it denotes, therefore, and marks that which follows the revelation of God in the Trinity, namely, *His creative works*. He is known by the things that are seen. Hence the written revelation commences with the words, "In the-beginning God CREATED." Creation is therefore the next thing-the *fourth* thing, and the number *four* always has reference to all that is *created*. It is emphatically the *number of creation*; of man and his relation to the world as created; while six is the number of man in his opposition to and independence of God. It is the number of things that have a beginning, of things that are made, of material things, and matter itself. It is the number of *material completeness*. Hence it is the world number, and especially the city number.

Four in contrast with seven: *Seven* stamps everything with *spiritual* perfection, for it is the number of heaven, and stands therefore in contrast to the earth. Hence, when in Rev. 5:12 the heavenly multitudes praise, they praise with a *seven-*fold blessing, and say: "Worthy is the Lamb that was slain to receive (1) power, and (2) riches, and (3) wisdom, and (4) strength, and (5) honour, and (6) glory, and (7) blessing."

Whereas, in v.13, (Rev.) When the created earthly beings praise,- the creatures that are "on the earth, and under the earth, and such as are in the sea, and all that are in them"- when these join in their ascription, it is only *four-fold*:- (1)"Blessing, and (2) honour, and (3) glory, and, (4) power, be unto Him that sitteth upon the throne, and unto the Lamb for ever and ever."

FIVE: (pgs. 135,136)

Five is four *plus* one (4+1=5). We have had hitherto the three persons of the Godhead, and their manifestation in creation. Now we have a further revelation of a People called out from mankind, redeemed and saved, to walk with God from earth to heaven. Hence, Redemption follows creation. Inasmuch as in consequence of the fall of man creation came under the curse and was "made subject to vanity," therefore man and creation must be redeemed. Thus we have:
1. Father.
2. Son.
3. Spirit.
4. Creation.
5. Redemption.
These are the five great mysteries, and *five* is therefore the number of **GRACE**.

If four is the number of the world, then it represents man's weakness, and helplessness, and vanity, as we have seen. But four *plus* one (4+1=5) is significant of Divine strength added to and made perfect in that weakness; of omnipotence combined with the impotence of earth; of Divine *favour* uninfluenced and indivincible.

Grace means favour. But what kind of favour? For favour is of many kinds. Favour shown to the miserable we call mercy; favour shown to the poor we call pity; favour shown to the suffering we call compassion; favour shown to the obstinate we call patience: but favour shown to the unworthy we call **GRACE!**

SIX: (pg.150)

Six is either 4 *plus* 2, *i.e.,* man's world (4) with man's enmity to God (2) brought in: or it is 5 *plus* 1, the grace of God made of none effect by man's addition to it, or perversion, or corruption of it: or it is 7 *minus* 1, *i.e.,* man's coming short of spiritual perfection. In any case, therefore, it has to do with *man;* it is the number of MAN as destitute of God, without God, without Christ.

SEVEN: (pgs.158,167,168)

We come now to the great number of *spiritual perfection.* A number which, therefore occupies so large a place in the works, and especially in the Word of God as being inspired by the Holy Spirit.

In the Hebrew, *seven* is (*shevah*). It is from the root (*savah*), *to be full* or *satisfied, have enough of.* Hence the meaning of the word "seven" is dominated by this root, for on the *seventh* day God rested from the work of Creation. It was full and complete, and good, and perfect. Nothing could be added to or taken away from it without marring it.

It is *seven*, therefore, that stamps with perfection and completeness that in connection with which it is used. Of *time*, it tells of the Sabbath, and marks off the week of seven days, which, artificial as it may seem to be, is universal and immemorial in its observance amongst all nations and in all times. It tells of that eternal Sabbath-keeping which remains for the people of God in all its everlasting perfection.

In the creative works of God, seven completes the colours of the spectrum and rainbow, and satisfies in music the notes of the scale.

Another meaning of the root (*Shavagh*) is *to swear,* or

make an oath. It is clear from the first occurrence in Gen. 21:31, "They sware both of them," that this oath was based upon the "seven ewe lambs" (vv.28,29,30), which point to the idea of *satisfaction* or *fullness* in an *oath*. It was the *security, satisfaction*, and *fullness* of the obligation, or completeness of the bond, which caused the same word to be used for both the number seven and an oath; hence it is written, "an oath for confirmation is an end to all strife." Beer-*sheba, the well of the oath*, is the standing witness of the spiritual perfection of the number *seven*.

EIGHT: (pgs.196, 200)

In Hebrew the number eight is (*Sh'moneh*), from the root (*Shah'meyn*), "to make fat," "cover with fat," "to super-abound." As a participle it means "one who abounds to strength," etc. As a noun it is "superabundant fertility," "oil," etc. So that as a numeral it is the super-abundant number. As *seven* was so called because the seventh day was the day of completion and rest, so *eight*, as the eighth day, was over and above this perfect completion, and was indeed the *first* of a new series, as well as being the *eighth*. Thus it already represents two numbers in one, the *first* and *eighth*.

It is 7 *plus* 1. Hence it is the number specially associated with *Resurrection* and *Regeneration*, and the beginning of a new era or order.

When the whole earth was covered with the flood, it was Noah "the eighth person" (2 Pet. 2:5) who stepped out onto a new earth to commence a new order of things. "Eight souls" (1 Pet. 3:20) passed through it with him to the new or regenerated world.

Hence too, circumcision was to be performed on the *eighth* day (Gen. 17:12), because it was the foreshadowing of the true circumcision of the heart, that which was to be "made without hands," even "the putting off of the body of the sins of the flesh by the circumcision of Christ" (Col. 2:11). This is connected with the new creation.

The first-born was to be given to Jehovah on the eighth day (Ex.22:29-30).

But, Resurrection is the great truth which is signified. Christ rose from the dead on "the *first* day of the week," that was of necessity the *eighth* day.

NINE: (pg. 235)

The number *nine* is a most remarkable number in many respects. It is held in great reverence by all who study the occult sciences; and in mathematical science it possesses properties and powers which are found in no other number.

It is the *last* of the digits, and thus marks the *end;* and is significant of the *conclusion* of a matter.

It is akin to the number *six*, six being the sum of its factors (3x3=9, and 3+3=6), and is thus significant of the *end of man*, and the summation of all man's works.

Nine is, therefore The Number of Finality or Judgment, for judgment is committed unto Jesus as "the Son of Man" (John 5:27; Acts 17:31). It marks the completeness, the end and issue of all things as to man- the judgment of man and all his works.

TEN: (pg. 243)

It has been already pointed out that *ten* is one of the perfect numbers, and signifies *the perfection of the Divine order*, commencing, as it does, an altogether new series of numbers. The first decade is the representative of the whole numeral system, and originates the system of calculation called "decimals," because the whole system of numeration consists of so many tens, of which the first is a type of whole.

Completeness of order, marking the entire round of anything, is, therefore, the ever-present signification of the number *ten*. It implies that nothing is wanting; that the number and order are perfect; that the whole cycle is complete.

ELEVEN: (pg. 251)

If *ten* is the number which marks the perfection of Divine *order*, then *eleven* is an *addition* to it, subversive of and undoing that order. If *twelve* is the number which marks the perfection of Divine *government*, then eleven falls short of it. So that whether we regard it as being 10+1, or 12-1, it is the number which marks *disorder, disorganization, imperfection*, and *disintegration*.

TWELVE: (pg. 253)

Twelve is a perfect number, signifying *perfection of government*, or of *governmental perfection*. It is found as a multiple of all that has to do with *rule*. The sun which "rules" the day, and the moon and stars which "govern" the night, do so by their passage through the *twelve* signs of the Zodiac which complete the great circle of the heavens of 360(12x30) degrees or divisions, and thus govern the year.

THIRTEEN: (pg. 205)

As to the significance of *thirteen*, all are aware that it has come down to us as a number of ill-omen. Many superstitions cluster around it, and various explanations are current concerning them.

Unfortunately, those who go backwards to find a reason seldom go back far enough. The popular explanations do not, so far as we are aware, go further back than the Apostles. But we must go back to *the first occurrence* of the number *thirteen* in order to discover the key to its significance. It occurs first in Gen. 14:4, where we read "*Twelve* years they served Chedorlaomer, and the *thirteenth* year they REBELLED."

Hence every occurrence of the number thirteen, and likewise of every multiple of it, stamps that with which it stands in connection with *rebellion, apostasy, defection, corruption, disintegration, revolution*, or some kindred idea.

NINETEEN: (pg. 262)

Nineteen is a number not without significance. It is a combination of 10 and 9, and would denote the perfection of *Divine order* connected with *judgment*. It is the *gematria* of Eve and Job.

Bullinger, E. W., Number in Scripture, published 1967 by Kregel Publications, P.O. Box 2607, Grand Rapids, MI 49501

Index of Scriptures:

81:12
103:10,11,12
119:127,128
128:3
Proverbs:
3:1,2,3,4,5,6,7,31
4:9,10
5:3,4,5,15,18,19
6:20,21,22,23
9:12
10:1
12:4
14:30
15:3,18,27
16:7,32
18:8,9,22
19:11,13,14,15
20:11
21:2,25,26
22:1
23:20,21
25:21,22
26:16
31:1,10,11,12,13,14,15,16,17
,18,19,20,21,22,23,24,25,26,
27,28,29,30,31
Ecclesiastes:
4:4,9
5:4,5
9:9
12:13
Isaiah:
5:20
14:12,13,14,15,16,17
45:22,23
53:4,5,6,10,11,12
54:17
55:8,9
56:11

64:4,6
Jeremiah:
17:9,10
20:9
Ezekiel:
22:12,13
28:12,13,14,15,16,17,18,19
Daniel:
5:20
Joel:
2:28
Zechariah:
3:1
Malachi:
2:14b
Matthew:
4:1,2,3,4,5,6,7,8,9,10,11
5:10,12,13,14,28,32,39,40,41
42,43,44
6:1,2,3,4,5,6,7,8,14,15,24,25,
26,27,28,29,30,31,32,33,34
7:3,14,21,22,23
9:37,38
10:7,8,9,10,11,12,13,14,15,
16,37
11:2,3,4,5,6
12:36,37
14:3,4,5,6,7,8,9,10,11,12
15:8,9,33
16:13,14,15,16,17,23,24,26
17:18,19,20,21
18:16
19:5
21:21,28,29,30,31
22:9,10,37
23:5,6,7,11,12,13,14,15,27,
28
25:41
27:46

Mark:
1:12,13,25,34,39
5:25,26,27,28,29,30,31,32,33
,34
6:11,14,15,16,17,18,19,20,21
,23,24,25,26
9:23
10:7,8,9,12
15:10,15,34
16:15,16,17,18
Luke:
1:17,37
3:19,20
4:1,2,3,4,5,6,7,8,9,10,11,12,
13,24,41
5:16
6:12
7:18,19,20,21,22,23
8:13
9:5,42
10:1,18,19
11:24,25,26
12:4,5
14:23
15:17a
17:3,4
18:10,11,12,13,14,27
22:31,32
23:44
John:
1:2,14
4:24
5:32
6:66
8:44
10:10,27,30
13:2
14:6,15
15:18,19

Acts:
5:1,2,3,4,5,6,7,8,9,10
8:7,27
16:16,17,18
18:2,18,26
21:9
Romans:
3:23
5:8
6:23
7:2,3
8:14,15,16,17,18,22,26,28,31
,35,36,37,38,39
10:12,13
12:2,12,14,16,20
14:2
16:3,4,20
1 Corinthians:
2:9
3:7
6:9,10,11,18
7:2,3,4,5,10,11,34,39,40
11:3,5,6,7,8,9,10,11,12,13,14
,15
12:13,14,15,16,17,18,19,20,
21,22,23,24,25,26,27
14:11,33,34,35
16:3,19
2 Corinthians:
1:3,4,5
2:11
4:10
5:17
9:7
10:4,5
11:3,14,15
12:9
13:1
Galatians:

185

Bibliography

The Holy Bible, King James Version, copyright 1901 by Louis Klopsch, printed by World Syndicate Company, Inc.; New York, NY

Scofield, C.I., *The Scofield Study Bible; King James Version,* published 1909, Oxford University Press; New York, NY

Weymann, Dorothy Mason, *Thus Saith God's Word,* published 1977, by MD Productions; Greensboro, NC

Wright, H. Norman, *Questions Women Ask in Private,* published 1993, Regal Books; Ventura, Ca.

Lockyer, Herbert, *All the Women of the Bible,* published by Zondervan Press; Grand Rapids, Mich.

Deans, Edith, *All the Women of the Bible,* published 1955, by Castle Books; Edison, NJ

Rawlings, Maurice S. MD., *To Hell and Back,* published 1993, Thomas Nelson Publishers; Nashville, TN.

MacArthur, John, *Guidelines for Singleness and Marriage,* published 1986, Moody Press; Chicago, Ill.

Morris, Henry M., *The Genesis Record,* published 1976, Baker Book House; Grand Rapids, Mich.

Morris, Henry M., *The Remarkable Record of Job,* published 1988, Baker Book House; Grand Rapids, Mich.

Chaffer, Lewis Sperry, *The Epistle to the Ephesians,* published 1991, Kregel Publications; Grand Rapids, Mich.

Scott, John R. W., *The Message of Ephesians,* published 1979, Inter-Varsity Press, Leicester, England; Downers Grove, Ill.

Guthrie, Donald, *The Pastoral Epistles* (The Tyndale New Testament Commentaries), published 1957, Wm. B. Eerdmans Publishing Company; Grand Rapids, Mich.

Allen, Tom, *Congregations in Conflict*, published 1991, Christian Publications; Camphill, Pa.

Thibon, Gustave, *What God Has Joined Together*, published 1952, Henry Regnery Company; Chicago, Ill.

Halley, Henry, H., *Halley's Bible Handbook*, published 1927 Zondervan Publishing; Grand Rapids, Mich.

Gordon, Robert, P., *1 & 2 Samuel*, published 1988, Regency Reference Library; Zondervan Publishing House; Grand Rapids, Mich.

Green, J.P. Sr., *The Interlinear Bible,* published 1976, by Hendrickson Publishers

Strong, James, LL.D., ST.D, *The New Strong's Exhaustive Concordance of the Bible,* published by Thomas Nelson Publishers; Nashville, Atlanta, London, Vancouver

Bullinger, E. W., *Number in Scripture*, published 1967, by Kregel Publications; Grand Rapids, Mich.

Bullinger, E.W., *Commentary on Revelation,* published 1984, Kregel Publications; Grand Rapids, Mich.

Funk & Wagnall, *Funk & Wagnall's New Standard Encyclopedia of Universal Knowledge,* published 1943, by Unicorn Press, New York, NY

Sumrall, Lester, *Pioneers of Faith*, published 1995, by Harrison House Books

Recommended Reading

Whyte, Maxwell H.A., *Power of the Blood,* published by Whitaker House

Madden, P.J., *The Wigglesworth Standard,* published by Whitaker House

Brown, Rebecca, M. D., *Prepare For War,* published by Whitaker House

MacArthur, John, *How to Meet the Enemy,* published by Victor Books

Somrall, Lester, *The Gifts and Ministries of the Holy Spirit,* published by Whitaker House

McGee, J. Vernon, *Through the Bible,* published by Thomas Nelson Publishers

Allen, Tom, *Congregations in Conflict,* published by Christian Publications

Bullinger, E.W., *Word Studies on the Holy Spirit,* published by Kregel Publications

Bullinger, E.W., *Great Cloud of Witnesses,* published by Kregel Publications

Pink, Arthur W., *The Antichrist,* published by Kregel Publications

Chaffer, Lewis Sperry, *Satan: His Motives and Methods,* published by Kregel Publications

Rawlings, Maurice, M.D., *To Hell and Back,* published by Thomas Nelson Publishers

Hunt, Dave, and McMahan, T.A., *The New Spirituality,* published by Harvest House

Tippit, Sammy, *The Gathering Storm*, published by Moody Press

Mather, George A., and Nichols, Larry A., *Dictionary of Cults, Sects, Religions, and the Occult,* published by Zondervan Publishing House

Morris, Henry M., *The Remarkable Record of Job*, published by Baker Book House

Anderson, Neil T., *Setting your Church Free*, published by Regal Books

Phillips, Phil, and Robie, Joan Hake, *Halloween and Satanism*, published by Starburst Publishers

Davis, John Hywel, *The Life of Smith Wigglesworth*, published by Vine Books

Stone, Nathan, *Names of God*, published by Moody Press

Horton, T. C., and Hurlburt, Charles E., *Names of Christ*, published by Moody Press

Pritchard, Ray, *Names of the Holy Spirit,* published by Moody Press

Wigglesworth, Smith, *Ever Increasing Faith*, published by Gospel Publishing

Ankerberg, John, and Weldon, John, *The Coming Darkness,* published by Harvest House

James, William T. (General Editor), *Foreshocks of Antichrist,* published by Harvest House